CONTEMPORARY PROBLEMS
OF DEMOCRACY

CONTEMPORARY PROBLEMS OF DEMOCRACY

by

MARVIN ZIMMERMAN

Department of Philosophy
State University of New York at Buffalo

with an Introduction by
SIDNEY HOOK

HUMANITIES PRESS
New York   1972

Library of Congress Catalog Card Number 73-187521

SBN number 391 00223 6

CONTENTS

PREFACE

My main purpose in writing this book is to help clarify some of the vital political issues on the contemporary scene. In dialogues with students, colleagues, and the public, I have found that these problems are rarely thought through. They do not receive the logical analysis devoted to matters of far less urgency. Too often their subtle and complex nature is not fully appreciated. Frequently action is urged or taken with respect to them that is grossly oversimplified and reflects an evaluation that is primarily emotional rather than the outcome of critical judgment.

I also hope to demonstrate that the political philosopher has a role to play in helping to make intelligent decisions, as well as engaging in analysis. In addition to breaking a problem into its parts, it is important to reassemble them in the light of fundamental insights and proferred solutions. There are intelligent and unintelligent ways of taking Humpty Dumpty apart. Putting him together again is preferable to gazing at the broken pieces or wringing one's hands in despair. Though no final answers are offered, I hope this book will promote more fruitful ones.

MARVIN ZIMMERMAN

INTRODUCTION

by Sidney Hook, New York University

"Democracy Without Rhetoric" or "Toward the Understanding of Democracy" could well serve as titles of Dr.
Marvin Zimmerman's lucid analysis of the concept of democracy and some of its major problems. His analysis appears at
a time in the United States which is characterized by a striking paradox. From any reasonable historical perspective it is
hardly contestable that our culture today is marked by a
greater degree of political dissent, more widely shared and
exercised civil freedom, less racial and religious discrimination, and a broader democratic mass base and participation
than ever before since the founding of the Republic. In many
sectors of our political and social life more progress—even if
far from enough—has been achieved in the last decade than
in any previous decade including the thirties.

Nonetheless, at no time has the concept of democracy and
the judgment that the United States enjoys a democratic
political system, whatever improvements still remain to be
made, been under such fierce attack. Not even at the height
of the totalitarian critique of the United States, when Vish-
insky and Goebbels were pointing with scorn at class and
racial inequalities within the United States in order to blunt
the effect of the political terror in their respective countries,
has the indictment against the American political democratic
system been so fierce, so extreme, and so regardless of past
achievement and present possibilities of further achievement.
Whereas in the past this unmeasured denunciation was
coupled with an attempt to prove that communism or some
other variety of totalitarianism was "essentially" or "basically" more democratic than the United States, today it often
proceeds from premises that call the democratic conception
itself into question. It is disheartening to those who have

relied upon the educational process to contribute to an understanding of the ethics and logic of democracy that misunderstandings and distortions of some of its central notions today flourish most luxuriantly in the academic community.

There are several features of Dr. Zimmerman's analysis that recommend themselves by their relevance and suggestiveness to the current scene of intellectual confusion. He brings home in a forceful and persuasive way the indispensability of the formal procedures of democratic rule without overlooking the distinction between the legitimate functioning of democracy and its occasional bitter fruit. Almost every attack on democracy transforms this *distinction* between the legitimate functioning of democracy and its consequences into a *separation*. The most familiar form of this transformation is to argue that, since majority rule may sometimes be mistaken and since sometimes allegedly good results may ensue from a disregard or suppression of majority rule, these allegedly good results give a democratic character or a democratic justification to the regime or to the factional activity that has rejected the formally legitimate democracy. But Dr. Zimmerman makes clear that, although majority rule may sometimes be unenlightened, it is less likely in the course of affairs to be unenlightened than an undemocratic minority, and that, in these situations in which the majority does act in an unenlightened way, the principled democrat, as Justice Frankfurter once put it, appeals from an unenlightened majority to an enlightened one.

Allied to this misconception of the nature of the political democratic process is the view that in a politically democratic community all its major social, economic, and cultural institutions must function in a politically democratic way. It is often held that because, in political life, all those who are affected by political decisions should have a voice and vote in determining who is to make these decisions and for how long, therefore this must be true in every other institution of the democratic political society—each one is to count for one, and the direction of policy, or the choice of those entrusted with the formulation and execution of policy, rests on majority rule. But this by no means follows. In a democratic political community it is not true that the army, the church, the family, the school, the museum, the orchestra, the Department of Health, etc., must function in the same fashion as the political community and operate by the same principles. The army is organized to protect the democratic community, the school to develop and disseminate knowledge and to further the growth of its students, the orchestra to produce enjoyable music. It would be absurd to elect and dismiss officers, parents, teachers, and orchestra and museum leaders in the way we do our public officials.

To be sure there is a sense in which one can speak of the democratic spirit of an army, of the democratic family as opposed to the authoritarian family, of democracy in education in contradistinction to education with an elite or class bias. This conception is derived from the ethical notion of democracy as a way of life and is expressed as an equality of concern and of opportunity for all human beings to develop themselves to their fullest reach as persons or human beings. Because an institution functions in a democratic spirit, invites participation in the discussion of common problems, and never treats any of the human beings it serves or who serve it *merely* as a means, it cannot mechanically transplant the mechanisms of political democracy.

There is not a single contemporary issue analyzed by Dr. Zimmerman about which he does not have something illuminating to say. Perhaps his discussion of the complex and controversial issues of the relation between democracy and communism today may be taken as paradigmatic of his approach. He insists rightfully on the distinction between communism as an economic system and communism as a political system and denies that democracy implies or necessarily involves any particular economic system. He argues that one who is committed to democracy as a political system must be every whit as opposed to communist as to fascist versions of totalitarianism. This runs counter to some forms of liberalism, which I have elsewhere characterized as ritualistic liberalism in contradistinction to realistic liberalism; these are color-blind to communist totalitarianism and profess to take the rhetorical pronouncements of communist propaganda as evidence of the "ultimate" or "basic" democratic intentions of communist regimes. Individuals who scorn the attempts to use the phrasing of the legal documents of some Southern states about equality to deny the facts of racial discrimination and who even with a self-righteous and unhistorical absolutism tax the founders of the American Republic with insincerity and hypocrisy because the ideals of the Declaration of Independence were violated by existing practices will cite the ideological slogans, the programs and promises of communist totalitarian states as evidence of their progressive character and of their kinship with the democratic ethos.

To be sure, the opposition to all forms of totalitarianism by a democrat does not mean that an equation can be drawn among them as equally dangerous or threatening to world peace and the prospects of democratic survival. In defense of the democratic interest it may even be necessary sometimes to become a cobelligerent with one totalitarian power to prevent the world hegemony or conquest of another totalitarian power. A principled democrat could for a limited period make common cause with the ruthless dictatorship of Stalin to curb the momentarily greater threat of the Nazi dictatorship of Hitler. But what a principled and intelligent democrat will not and should not do is to deny the undemocratic and terrorist nature of the communist regime. The principled and intelligent democrat will not urge that it is the duty of democratic regimes to safeguard the liberties and independence of all peoples anywhere from totalitarian aggression of whatever character. But he does recognize the duty of sympathy and on occasion, even some material and psychological support, for a people struggling to preserve its liberties and independence from destruction at the hands of foreign totalitarian powers. The Spanish democratic republic went down to defeat because of the failure of European democratic regimes as well as the U.S. to provide it with means for its defense against the revolt of Franco backed by the massive and active intervention of Fascist Italy and Nazi Germany. Principles by themselves do not decide what the intelligent policy should be in specific situations but without them nations as well as individuals lapse into cynical opportunism relieved by occasional adventurism.

Dr. Zimmerman's analysis of the differences between democracy and communism today—which he justifiably characterizes as political and moral, and not economic, as concerned primarily with freedom of moral and political choice, and not the freedom of economic enterprise—should stand us in good stead today when diplomatic, cultural, and trade relations with Communist China are gradually being established. The illusions that for many years blinded the American intellectual community to the truths about the Soviet domestic terror, illusions that finally withered only after Khrushchev's revelations in 1956, are now being cultivated with respect to Communist China. The equivalents of Walter Duranty and the Sidney and Beatrice Webbs, without their great imaginative talents, have reappeared heralding the great advances achieved under Mao Tse-tung's rule. The impression is given that, even at a time when political and cultural repression has been intensified, the alleged economic gains of communist rule in some way reduces the abyss between the free and open society and the closed society. Any reader who has benefited from Dr. Zimmerman's demonstration that in a genuinely democratic society it is the mode of political decision, not the mode of economic production, that is decisive will not be taken in by the allegations that the Peking regime enjoys almost universal popular support. He will ask why, if there is such almost universal support, no opposition party, press, or even inner party faction is tolerated. He will ask why it is that, in the rare instances when Chinese are given a choice to remain or leave, they overwhelmingly rush pell-mell to flee the country. They will ask why freedom of movement within the country is severely controlled; why organized groups are permitted to function outside the law and even the party to destroy any elements in the population that the ruling hierarchy of the Communist Party seeks to crush; why the official glorification of the leader has reached a pitch of intensity that surpasses the adoration of Stalin at the height of his rule by terror.

These questions *mutatis mutandis* will be asked by principled and intelligent democrats about every communist regime in the world whether Cuba or North Viet Nam.

One final word: It should be clear that, despite his principled opposition to all forms of totalitarianism, Dr. Zimmerman is no defender of the social, political, or economic *status quo*. Were our choice restricted today, *as it is not*, between the *status quo* on the one hand and any form of totalitarianism on the other, all humane and intelligent persons would support the *status quo* instead of the programs of repression and terror advocated by the prophets of the new totalitarianism. But there is no *status quo!* Our choice lies between continuously expanding and strengthening democratic institutions, even as we defend them from attack, and seeking short cuts, under a variety of transparent rationalizations, that would achieve the "new," "the higher," "the directed," "the socialist democracy" of the future by destroying the democratic freedoms of the present. Dr. Zimmerman has presented a series of powerful arguments that will, one hopes, move readers to take a stand with him in behalf of the true permanent democratic revolution.

CONTEMPORARY PROBLEMS
OF DEMOCRACY

CHAPTER I

DEMOCRACY AND MAJORITY RULE*

I. Can Rule of the Majority Be Justified?

In endeavoring to justify majority rule over against minority rule in basic political affairs, I have deliberately refrained from using the terms "democracy" and "dictatorship" because of their highly ambiguous nature. However, it is frequently asked whether or not democracy can be vindicated. If this is meant in either the unlimited or limited sense of majority rule and if the subsequent analysis is sound, then I shall claim that democracy has been shown to be more desirable than any system characterized by minority rule (dictatorship, totalitarian state, etc.).

Even if one believes that the voice of the people is the voice of God, the majority of the people, it is universally admitted, may be wrong. Can majority rule be justified even though the majority often errs in what it approves? Since abilities and knowledge vary, and some judgments are obviously superior to others, are there a few, more capable than the majority, of rendering decisions beneficial to society?[1] It has been repeatedly pointed out that no minority can be entrusted to govern, given the selfish tendencies and corruptness of man. But, if true, is it not also true the majority are more encumbered with the liabilities flowing from additional numbers and a selfishness bridled by intelligence in shorter supply? Therefore, on balance, minority rule of the more competent might appear preferable. This conclusion is based on two assumptions: (1) that selfishness has no effect on capability, and (2) that both minority rule and majority rule are *equally* vulnerable to selfishness.

We are presupposing that capability here refers to the knowledge and ability necessary to rendering decisions beneficial to society. By selfishness we mean acting for one's own interest, regardless of others. Thus, the selfishness of a ruling minority, however proficient, would tend to inhibit it from making decisions in the interest of society as a whole particularly if and when such judgments conflict with its own interests. The very selfishness of the minority will tend to counteract the advantage of having a more capable ruling minority rather than a less capable ruling majority.

Granted the vulnerability to selfishness of a more capable ruling minority. Does selfishness render a less capable ruling majority equally vulnerable?

Selfishness implies acting for one's own interest, even at the expense of others. This means that a selfish ruling majority will tend to act in behalf of its own interest and will refrain from approving actions in the interest of others if they conflict with its own considered interest. But since the interest of society consists of the interest of all the people—the majority as well as others—a selfish ruling majority will tend to produce decisions favorable to a greater portion of society (the majority) than will a selfish ruling minority. Assuming then the degree of egoism to be the same in members of the majority and minority, there is less likelihood of the majority failing to regard the legitimate interests of citizens than the minority.

What about the factor of ability? A more capable minority can theoretically render decisions more favorable to a majority and can succeed more frequently in doing this than the majority can. But is such a minority willing to do this, particularly when contrary to its interest? Attempts are more likely to be made if one is willing than unwilling, and success appears more likely to occur if one tries than otherwise—this seems to hold even for psychotics, let alone normal humans. A selfish majority, though wishing to, will not always succeed in acting in its own interest. Perhaps it does not succeed too often. But this is preferable to almost never succeeding because one is unwilling though able.

Consequently, it seems that while neither ruling group

will act in the interest of the *whole* of society, majority rule will benefit a larger number than minority rule. Hence minority rule appears to be more vulnerable to selfishness than majority rule. Of course, human beings do not always act selfishly, even as rulers, and therefore some profit might accrue from a superior ruling minority. But it is also clear that human beings do not always act unselfishly; hence one can see the advantage of majority rule over minority rule. A difficulty arises in making an accurate assessment because most people seem to fall between the two extremes of complete selfishness and complete benevolence. Furthermore, people fluctuate in selfish tendencies and are affected differently when given authority. To complicate matters further, not every decision by a ruling power is equal in importance, whether motivated by selfishness or unselfishness. It appears difficult to judge the relative merits of the alternatives with any degree of precision. Nevertheless, I believe a rough assessment can be made. A perusal of the history of man and society will reveal that people generally are more egoistic than altruistic and thereby inclined to make more selfish decisions than unselfish ones. Whether we look at the deeds of Caesar, Napoleon and Hitler, labor unions, business and farm blocs, or the ordinary man in his search for survival, livelihood, and success, the evidence for this seems convincing.

Clearly "all history taught that all men alike were greedy of power and that none could be trusted with power. Kings and nobles, the church and the army, the rich and the powerful, all abused power; the people—in those fitful episodes when they happened to enjoy power—were equally wicked and despotic."[2]

It is not necessary for our argument to maintain that men are inherently or innately selfish, or to deny the possibility that humans could be conditioned to act altruistically. In the light of past experience, it is justifiable to conclude that it is highly improbable that men could or would be made unselfish.

It is interesting to find that Herbert Marcuse prefers rule

by an "elite" to rule by the "people" on the grounds that the latter, in contemporary societies, have been "brainwashed." Even so, on what grounds could he trust any "elite," however capable, not to resort to brainwashing of its own, in its own interest? He argues:

> If the final democratic criterion of the declared opinion of the majority no longer (or rather not yet) prevails, if vital ideas, values and ends of human progress no longer (or rather not yet) enter as competing equals, the formation of public opinion, if the people are no longer (or rather not yet) sovereign but "made" by the real sovereign powers—is there any alternative other than the dictatorship of an "elite" over the people? For the opinion of people (usually designated as The People) who are unfree in the very faculties in whch liberalism saw the roots of freedom: independent thought and independent speech, can carry no overriding validity and authority—even if The People constitute the overwhelming majority.[3]

This position had been stated long before Marcuse by Lenin and Stalin in justifying the view that the so-called "dictatorship of the proletariat" (which Marx interpreted by dubious extrapolation into the rule of the overwhelming majority and therefore democratic) could only function through the "dictatorship of the party"—a minority self-selected elite group.

Of course, it is compatible with democracy for a small group of well-intentioned and capable individuals to seize power in an undemocratic society and eventually transfer it to the people. But it is contrary to belief in majority rule to hold that the majority is too corrupt to correct itself through the democratic processes and needs to be "reconditioned" by an "enlightened elite" which could subsequently restore power to an "enlightened" and "rational" public. Marcuse supports this view in maintaining that the people, corrupted by capitalism, have continued by majority rule to perpetuate the corruption of future generations.

He assumes that values held by a majority in a democratic society are somehow immune to changes urged by "enlightened minorities," because popular and conventional opinion overwhelm the small, weak voice of reason and rational dissent. This position does not square with changes in public attitudes over long periods of time. Who are so "rational" and enlightened" that they cannot eventually win over a majority, as long as some kind of dissent is permitted? Perhaps what is described as "rational" and "enlightened" is not, or more time and effort are needed for reforms to become publicly acceptable. Surely the United States, England, France, Sweden, etc., are significantly different from what they were fifty years ago.

Possibly what Marcuse and others consider "rational" is incompatible with the nature of man and presupposes a completely benevolent humanity. Selfishness, corruption, benevolence, and kindness are all matters of degree, and they depend on the individuals and their activities, be they relatives, friends, and strangers, or sex, hunger, and self-preservation. Granted that human nature is not fixed, are there limits to its plasticity? Individuals vary in how far they can be pushed. Can all humans be conditioned to completely and permanently curb their drives of sex, hunger, and self-preservation?

Plato might have hoped that a group of wise philosopher kings could be molded who would transcend all personal desires, interests, and motivations, and lead an ideal society. But the history of man and his biology does not encourage the belief that such a state of affairs could be achieved, let alone sustained. Could such a group of "gods" provide for the benevolence and sanity of themselves and their replacements in all matters?

Even if certain social and economic values, systems, or institutions encourage more greediness and exploitation than might otherwise exist, it does not mean that men would become automatically or even more benevolent in their absence, particularly the minority elite who would wield authority. If somehow, most men could be conditioned to be benevolent, there would still be the problem of controlling those who supervised the conditioning and could exploit the benevolence of others. There would always be the problem raised by those who might not become benevolent under the conditioning or remain so if they did. However sincere and well-intentioned a group of individuals may be in believing that they have discovered the secret of reducing or eliminating man's selfishness, to transfer all power into their hands is to ask mankind to take the risk that their "cure" will succeed in removing the malady of selfishness long before they themselves succumb to it or their power falls into the hands of less scrupulous individuals. Unless it can be shown that men are inherently or innately benevolent or that it is highly probable that men will be conditioned to become benevolent, simple common sense nurtured by experience impell us to assume that people will continue to be more egoistic than altruistic.[4] As Sidney Hook points out: "Not a single benevolent act of a despot recorded in history but can be matched with scores of malevolent acts. For every guilty man a dictator spares there are thousands of innocent men he dooms."[5]

I believe this is true even for relatively unimportant decisions made by those not occupying posts of the ruling power. The tendency toward selfishness is accentuated as decisions become relatively more important. We may yield the right of way to others on secondary matters but not where our basic goods, our liberties, or our lives are at stake. The egoistic component in decision making grows even greater when made by those with stronger power in the ruling structure of society.

The "importance" of a decision refers to how beneficial or detrimental it tends to be to the individual members of society concerned or affected by its consequences. Thus a relatively important decision will be more beneficial or detrimental to them than a relatively unimportant one. The selfish tendency becomes greater where decisions become relatively more important because the more advantageous or detrimental to society a decision tends to be, the more there is at stake for the individual members of society, *i.e.*, the more there is to gain or lose in making that decision. The more there is to gain or lose, the more an individual will be inclined to support judgments beneficial to himself and to oppose those detrimental to himself. For example, assuming that an individual considers the consequences of the decisions beneficial to himself, he is more likely to uphold an important decision to support a war than an unimportant one to impose a tax for improving the scenery. Conversely, if he considers these decisions detrimental to himself, he is more likely to oppose the war than the tax.

A greater voice in society means more power and less vulnerability to the dictates of others, making it less necessary to be responsive to the interests and needs of others. There is less pressure to ameliorate or accommodate one's selfishness to others, and one is likely to be more selfish. As Sidney Hook asserts: "Taken literally, Lord Acton's maxim, 'Power always corrupts and absolute power corrupts absolutely,' is an exaggeration. But there is sufficient truth in it to give us pause when we are about to invest individuals or groups with great power, even temporarily."[6]

The conclusion we draw from the foregoing is that genuine majority rule will tend to be more advantageous to society than minority rule. If "justify" merely signifies the extent to which society is likely to benefit, there is greater justification for majority rule than minority rule. Because majority rule is a matter of degree, *i.e.*, a function of the extent to which a majority makes decisions, the greater the degree of majority rule, the greater its justification.

Our basic assumption, vindication of majority rule over minority rule on the grounds that the former is of greater benefit to society than the latter, will certainly be challenged. It may be argued that because something is more advantageous to society it does not follow that we ought to accept it, that it is preferable, or that it is justified. In effect, we are being accused of committing the "naturalistic" fallacy of defining ethical terms in a descriptive manner, *i.e.*, in utilitarian terms.[7] I accept the force of this objection against attempts to define ultimate value terms descriptively by discovering their "correct" definitions or uses. However, I am not suggesting that my use of these words represents the "correct" definition. I am offering a "stipulative" definition of terms such as "ought," "justify," and "preferable." In effect, all I mean by asking whether majority rule is "justified" is: Is it of greater benefit to society than minority rule? My contention is the hypothetical claim that, if one wishes to select a political system that will offer the greatest advantage to society, then majority rule will be chosen over minority rule.

I have selected this stipulative definition because I have found that people more frequently argue or debate issues of a social, political, and ethical nature with this kind of criteria presupposed, *i.e.*, the "public interest," the "good of society," the "greatest happiness for the greatest number," and similar locutions, than with other kinds of ultimate values.

That majority rule is "justified" in my sense leaves it open for anyone to maintain that majority rule is not "justified" in some other sense, but that is an entirely different consideration. If one wishes to challenge my contention that majority rule is justified, it will be appropriate to disprove my belief that majority rule is of greater benefit to society than any alternative system.

II. *Can Limits to Majority Rule Be Justified?*

Does majority rule presuppose either the paradoxical right of a majority to abolish majority rule, or the paradoxical right to prohibit the majority from doing this? If majority rule is the preferred means of benefiting society in the long run, then we are concerned with permanent majority rule, not temporary majority rule. However this precludes the right of a majority to abolish majority rule since granting this right could result in eliminating permanent majority rule, whereas prohibiting this right would not.

The problem of preventing a temporary majority from abolishing majority rule raises a number of interesting questions. If a temporary majority can abolish it legally, one can perhaps justify illegal action (civil disobedience and revolution) to prevent or reverse this. If one wishes to make it illegal to abolish majority rule, then some machinery is needed which is not subject to the will of any majority at any particular time. There are important questions here concerning the extent to which totalitarian political parties and organizations can be allowed to function and grow in a democratic society.

In any case, the claim that people have a right to choose any form of government they wish, even one which does away with the right of the people to choose any form of government they wish, is on the face of it self-contradictory; by qualifying the right of the people at any particular time to restrict the right of people at some future time to choose, the contradiction can be resolved. In effect to talk about democracy and rule by the people as desirable is to talk presumably about a long-run, permanent political system. It is to refer to a continuous process of choices and decision making by a continuous and permanent series of nominations, elections, secret ballots, etc., and the like, that make up the democratic ideology. If this is what is meant by democracy, then in the name of democracy a majority of the people do not have the right to do away with it.

Having granted one restriction on the majority, are there other similarly justified restraints, e.g., restrictions incorporated in a constitution, the bill of rights, or judicial review? Do the latter restrictions serve the same purpose as the former one, i.e., maintain permanent majority rule? Are these latter curbs presupposed by permanent majority rule?

If a majority were to deprive a minority of parts of the bill of rights, e.g., the right of free speech or press, it would not seem to prevent permanent majority rule. Furthermore, if the majority were prohibited from doing this, permanent majority rule would be impeded in these areas. Yet we believe that these latter restrictions on the majority are justified. Can we reconcile this with our defense of permanent majority rule?

"If the majority may use government to do its will, is that not an attack upon the inalienable rights of men over against government? If there are limits upon what government may do, is that not a challenge to or even a denial of the principle of majority rule? Here is a paradox not yet resolved in our political philosophy or our constitutional system."[8] If we accept the latter restrictions, then our position has been qualified, for we are now implying that majority rule is not best in *all* matters. How does one determine which affairs are to be decided by the majority and which are not?

Our original reason for preferring majority rule is predicated on the belief that people tend to act on the basis of self-interest. But would this also apply to decisions prohibited by the above restrictions? Would permitting the majority the right to limit free speech, on the basis of self-interest, tend to benefit society, whereas restricting the majority have the contrary effect?

We believe that a majority acting on the basis of self-interest does not always further its own welfare, and would have the opposite effect if it decided to limit free speech. But doesn't this also apply to all majority decisions?

Perhaps believing a majority does not *always* promote its own advantage, is compatible with preferring majority rule over minority rule on the grounds that the former is *more likely* to advance its own interest than the latter. Minority rule would give the minority power to act in its own interest at the expense of the majority by preventing the majority from making decisions. This kind of limitation of the majority is different from the restrictions above (bill of rights) in that the latter also restrains the minority. The latter restrictions apply to all individuals, minority as well as majority, in the interest of all individuals, and this is quite different from limitations of a majority by a minority to the advantage of the minority only. On the other hand, it might be claimed that the distinction between these two kinds of restrictions is a distinction without a difference. The latter restrictions have the practical effect of satisfying the wishes of any minority who might otherwise be prevented from the exercise of free speech by a majority. In effect, this would constitute minority rule where the wishes of a majority are curbed by the latter restrictions.

The original objection to minority rule was that it would promote its interest at the expense of the majority. But it doesn't follow that every judgment desired by a minority advances its interest at the expense of the majority, particularly if the minority does not make that decision. The latter restrictions (bill of rights) appear to exemplify that kind of decision which, though desired by the minority, is not made by it. If the latter restrictions satisfied the minority and displeased the majority by protecting the former from being excluded by the latter in the exercise of certain rights, the reverse is also true. It would also satisfy the majority and displease the minority by safeguarding the former from being excluded by the latter.

Presumably decisions involving conflicting interests, where promoting the interest of the minority would be harmful to the interest of the majority, ought to be made by the majority. A tax law which benefits the majority at the expense of the minority might very well qualify as an example. On the other hand, judgments involving shared interests, where advancing the interest of a minority would also benefit the majority, would seem to warrant enactment without regard to majority rule. Freedom of speech, for example, would benefit both minority and majority.

Clearly, "any legislation which sets arbitrary limits to inquiry or discussion is treason to democracy not only—not even primarily—because it impairs minority rights, but because it denies to the majority itself that weapon without which democracy is paralyzed and impotent."[9] Of course, there will be disagreements about which interests conflict and which do not. It cannot be assumed that these kinds of disputes ought to be resolved by majority rule. Who is to determine which restrictions will be placed upon majority rule? If a majority decides to limit itself, then this does not restrict majority rule, but rather reflects it. In such a case, the majority has not been prohibited from limiting the rights of a minority, but has approved of granting it such rights. On the other hand, only if a minority is authorized to set limits will the majority be subject to restrictions. The judgment as to whether these prohibitions benefit society will be in the hands of the minority. If this minority can make these decisions, without regard to, or contrary to, the wishes of the majority, we run the risk of a minority acting in its own interests, contrary to the interests of the majority. Sidney Hook states it cogently: "But if the rights of individuals are not safe in the hands of a majority, are they any safer in the hands of a minority? Who is to select the minority, and how are the rights of the majority to be safeguarded against the minority?"[10]

Our justification for majority rule is that the majority is more likely to act in its own interest. If on occasion it acts contrary to its own welfare, is it not likely to change its policies?

"Granted that majorities—like courts—are liable to error, how is that error to be cured and how is the repetition of that error best to be awarded? Is it not reasonable to suppose that majorities, like individuals, learn by their mistakes, and that only the lessons learned by experience make a lasting impression?"[11]

Our objection to minority rule is that it is more likely to act against the interest of the majority. If on occasion the minority acts to the advantage of the majority, is it not likely to eventually act to the contrary? We must remember that the members of any majority or minority are continually changing. If it is beneficial to society for a majority not to curtail freedom of speech, it does not mean that it is beneficial to society for a majority not to have the power to do so. It is also of advantage that free speech not be limited by a minority. If the majority is not to have the authority to limit free speech, then a minority will have to be assigned the right to prevent it. In effect, this gives the minority the power to limit it.

It will be said that no one should have the power to limit freedom of speech, neither a minority nor a majority, and that some basic legal structure such as the Bill of Rights be instituted which constitutes a restriction against all groups from violating this fundamental right. But who will insure that this restriction is sustained? If we give this power to a judicial body such as the Supreme Court, which is not subject to majority rule, then in effect what remains is rule by a minority.

"Nevertheless, it is true that Supreme Court justices are not directly responsible to the people in the sense that elected officials are, and it is equally obvious that government by nine specialists, appointed for life and at least theoretically insulated from the political process, smacks of something other than democracy."[12]

It may be suggested that this judicial body will not have the power to limit freedom of speech, but only the right to constrain any majority or minority from doing so. It will also be said that the very basic restriction, the Bill of Rights, will make it clear that no one, including the judicial body, has the power to limit freedom of speech. However, it is this body which will interpret and apply this basic restriction. In practice, this body may circumscribe freedom of speech, for it can decide whether any minority or majority has violated the restriction. It will have the power to interpret the law so that, in effect, it limits the freedom of speech of a minority or majority, or allows a minority or majority to limit someone else's freedom of speech. The authority given this body will extend to other basic freedoms or rights and to any conflicts arising among them. Even those areas which belong to the jurisdiction of the majority and are not part of the basic freedoms or rights in need of protection from majority abuse will be in danger of being interpreted as part of the basic rights.

"With this freedom of maneuver, judges can invade the arena of political decision-making, and the history of American constitutional law is marked by vigorous instances of such intervention."[13] Thus, this minority will have the power to extend its jurisdiction to any and all areas belonging to the majority. As Sidney Hook declares:

> Conceive as sharply as you please the line of distinction between economic legislation which affects the complex of strategic human freedoms and economic legislation which does not and is concerned merely with differing economic arrangements. It is still within the power of the justices of the Court to draw that line in practice—whether with easy abandon or sober restraint. No one knows how they will do it and when. All that can be known is that the doctrine of judicial supremacy gives them, and justifies giving them, the power to do it, that in exercising this power the Court often acts as a third and superior legislative chamber, and that the extent to which it uses the power it has depends upon the changing composition of the Court, upon the backgrounds, philosophies, and personalities of the individual justices.[14]

Indeed, we are faced with the dilemma of majority rule versus minority rule. We recognize that majority rule is preferable, but there are certain basic rights we wish to protect from abuse by the majority. However, in order to effectively restrict the majority, we run the risk of abuse by minority rule, not only over basic rights but all other areas as well.

"If there are no limits to the power of the majority, minorities could disappear. Somewhere a limit must be set on what a majority can do. Otherwise, it can ride roughshod over all opposition. When the minority is adequately protected, however, it may be able to prevent the majority from accomplishing anything positive."[15] Our very justification for majority rule indicates that, in all areas (the basic rights as well as other matters), the danger of abuse resulting from majority rule is a lesser evil than that of minority rule.

Even if freedom of speech is beneficial to society, it doesn't follow that it always is for all people, or in every subject matter or at all times.

"The Fifth and Fourteenth Amendments guarantee the citizen due process of law in language no less demanding that that in which the First Amendment guarantees free speech. If a newspaper in the course of a trial uses its First Amendment freedoms to attempt to intimidate judge and jurors, there is obviously a conflict between two equally protected rights which cannot be solved by trumpeting about the glories of free speech."[16] No freedom or right is absolute, for it may conflict with other freedoms or rights in certain situations. As Sidney Hook forcefully reasons:

> If freedom of speech, as it sometimes does, prejudices or imperils a man's right to a fair trial (not to speak of cases when it threatens a man's right to life—for example, when a mob is being incited to a lynch), how can *both* be absolute or unqualified? What happens when the right to property conflicts with the right to safety, the right to education, the right to defense (and the complex cluster of rights implied in the very preamble of the Constitution)? When freedom of press grievously violates the right to privacy, which is to yield to which and under what conditions? The right to tax is not necessarily a power to destroy, but it certainly is a power to abridge property and redistribute wealth. In morals, one good or right limits another: can it be any different in political life or in any intelligent construction of constitutional law?[17]

But even if freedom of speech is an absolute, there appears to be a greater danger to society in entrusting the power to protect or regulate this right to a minority rather than a majority. However, it is compatible with majority rule for the majority to pass laws protecting freedom of speech and to delegate power to a judicial body to guard this freedom. At the same time, the majority would have the power to override judicial findings, thereby avoiding the danger of minority decisions over which it had no control. Even if a majority should desire to curb freedoms, the legislative process in changing laws or overriding judicial decisions would allow opportunity for hearing objections to limiting these freedoms, in the same way as other kinds of legislation.

It should be noted that "A good part of our politics, indeed, seems to be concerned with reconciling majority and minority will, class hostilities, sectional differences, the divergent interests of producer and consumer, of agriculture and labor, of creditor and debtor, of city and country, of taxpayer and tax-beneficiary, of the military and the civilian. In small issues as in great, the result is generally a compromise. Democracy, in short, whether from instinct or from necessity, furnishes its own checks and balances—quite aside from such as may be provided in written constitutions."[18]

It is not difficult to cite undesirable instances of judicial review. "Pollock v. Farmers' Loan and Trust Co. invalidated the income-tax law of 1894. It remains, with Dred Scott, the most unfortunate of all exhibitions of judicial review. The opinion reversed earlier decisions and was, in turn, reversed by the Sixteenth Amendment. Its practical effect was merely to delay for almost twenty years the application of a system of taxation universally recognized as sound."[19]

It may be argued that recently, at least, the Supreme Court has done more to protect freedom of speech than would have been the case if the Court had been subject to majority rule. It has apparently broadened or extended these rights rather than restricted them, though it has had the power to do otherwise.

But not all these decisions have been beneficial to society, not all have been opposed by a majority, and not all have broadened rather than restricted basic rights. Some decisions which have extended certain basic rights have curtailed other basic rights or the basic rights of others, which are equally if not more important. Some decisions have not been opposed by the majority. On the contrary, if we judge by laws passed by federal and state legislative bodies, they have been supported by the elective process most closely associated with majority rule. Many decisions have been neither supported nor resisted by the majority, but have been supported or opposed by certain minorities. There is no reason to believe, therefore, that these decisions would be overruled by the majority even if it had the power to do this. In a number of instances, even in recent times (and more often prior to the New Deal), the decisions restricted basic rights in an undesirable manner. As Hook wisely declares: "A sober and unbiased reading of judicial nullifications of Congressional legislation will show that on the whole they have been more clearly motivated by a desire to preserve the rights of private property from popular demands for social welfare and social justice than by a fervent belief in the ideals of personal freedom and equality."[20]

But even where decisions were desirable and contrary to majority approval, we are obliged to consider the long run consequence of giving the Court unlimited power to make rulings opposed by a majority, rather than attempting to persuade a majority to accept decisions we believe desirable. As already indicated, this power is not limited to judgments we happen to prefer, but also those we find unpalatable, including those which go beyond the area of basic rights. A long-run calculation of the consequences of unrestricted judicial review must also include an evaluation of the bitterness, frustration, and evasion of the majority subject to decisions to which it is opposed and which it cannot change. Part of the calculation of whether a judgment is beneficial to society is whether the majority believes it is. If the majority thinks otherwise, it detracts from an otherwise beneficial decision. Commager points out that "most of the judicial nullifications of federal legislation have been cancelled out by amendment, by new —and more acceptable—legislation, or, more frequently, by judicial reversal."[21]

He adds, later on: "Almost every instance of judicial nullification of congressional acts appears, now, to have been a mistaken one. In many—perhaps in most—instances the mistake has been (after a decent interval) conceded and corrected by the court itself. In other instances it has been rectified by the operation of public opinion. The conclusion is almost inevitable that judicial review in this realm has been a drag upon administrative efficiency and upon democracy."[22]

Let us suppose the majority desires to limit the free speech of communists and fascists. At present the majority does not have the power to overrule the Supreme Court's decisions protecting that right. Is this more beneficial to society in the long run than the possession of that power by the majority? While we recognize the advantages of the right of free speech for minorities, we tend to overlook the harm if a majority believes otherwise. This would not only displease the majority but encourage them to resist, evade, and circumvent implementation of the Supreme Court's decisions.

We are also inclined to overstate the advantage of not restricting free speech by presupposing that society will be willing to hear these minorities and thus benefit from unlimited free speech. But if a majority really believes that free speech for these minorities is harmful it is not likely to listen to them. It is more likely to be hostile to their ideas expressed through the exercise of free speech. Furthermore, we need to distinguish between curtailing free speech of a few, and ultimately restricting others as well. Some assume that restriction of a few will lead to restriction of others and thus overstate the dangers. Though possible, a majority is not likely to support curbs which apply to itself; on the contrary, one reason the majority will cite in support of restricting the few is the belief (however mistaken) that the few would endanger the rights (including free speech) of the majority.

"It is always easy to be in favor of free speech when the

speaker is saying something harmless or something with which we agree. The real problem of the First Amendment comes when the speaker is expressing ideas we hate or fear, or is speaking in the hope of destroying the freedom of others."[23] The tendency to exaggerate the benefits and overlook the harm from restricting majority rule apply similarly to other basic rights, and here too a case for majority rule can be made.

In the United States, two major obstacles to majority rule have been the principle of judicial review and the Constitutional amending process. Supreme Court members are appointed for life and their decisions cannot be set aside by a simple majority.

"Federal judges obviously have exercised political functions, yet in the technical sense they are wholly irresponsible, i.e., they are appointed for life and are in no way responsible to the people for their actions. The only checks on judicial actions are latent: the possibility of impeachment, a congressional decision to limit federal jurisdiction, and the graveyard. Except for cases of clear criminal behavior, impeachment is a dead letter."[24] A mere majority cannot amend the Constitution. "But it takes more than a majority to amend a constitution or to write a new one, and under our present system a determined minority can, if it will, effectively veto any change in the federal document and in most state documents."[25] A majority could be authorized to overturn Supreme Court findings and to amend the Constitution. Thus, it is unnecessary to dispose of either judicial review or the amending process.

Although our defense of majority rule has been confined primarily to the unlimited sense, it also constitutes a defense of limited majority rule over minority rule since the extent to which society benefits is a function of the extent to which the majority participates in ruling.

III. *What Does Majority Rule Imply?*

We originally argued that majority rule in the long run is inconsistent with any majority abrogating majority rule. This raises the important question whether there are other decisions incompatible with majority rule in the long run, for example, to restrict the right of minorities to vote. Countries acknowledged to be democratic or characterized by majority rule generally lay down such voting qualifications as age, residence, and literacy requirements. We may grant that certain voting restrictions are compatible with majority rule on the grounds that voting presupposes a minimum amount of knowledge and experience. However, who is to decide criteria for voting? Surely it is possible for a minority to deprive a majority of the right to vote.

Since justification of majority rule was based primarily on self-interest, it is plausible to restrict the voting right to the adult population who would represent the self-interest of the nonadult population on the basis of parental ties. Majority rule would consist of a majority of the total adult population having the determining voice in running society. But would it be compatible with majority rule to deprive a minority of the adult population of the right to vote?

Majority rule implies that, where differences exist, the will of a majority shall prevail. But if only a majority can vote, there will be cases where it will split into two groups each of which will constitute a minority of the original total voting population. Here it will be impossible to determine the will of the majority of the original total voting population, and thus impossible to have majority rule. In effect, minority rule will result, since the position of the larger of the two minority groups will prevail. We conclude, therefore, that excluding a minority of the adult population from the right to vote is incompatible with majority rule in the long run.

Are there other basic rights which, if removed from a minority, would be incompatible with majority rule in the long run, *e.g.*, the right of free speech? Clearly "the rights guaranteed by the First Amendment are essential to the exercise of all other rights, and enjoy therefore a preferred position in the Constitution. Majorities may be permitted to make mistakes elsewhere, but not here, for mistakes here might undermine and destroy the very principle of majority rule."[26] It will be argued that the right to vote carries with it the right of any minority to speak and persuade others to vote in the same way. Otherwise, the right to vote itself becomes an exercise in futility. Similar arguments could be elicited for other basic rights. Sidney Hook maintains: "Even when elections or plebiscites are held without overt terror or the constraining presence of the military and police, they cannot be accepted as evidence that they reflect the judgment of the electorate if there is no freedom of speech, press, assembly, and especially the *rights of opposition*."[27]

However, we need to distinguish between those conditions that are logically implied by majority rule, and those that are not, however desirable they may be. Otherwise we may think that all legislation beneficial to society, such as welfare, medical aid, unemployment insurance, and education, which contributes to better decision making by the voting population, is logically implied by majority rule. Sidney Hook argues persuasively:

> It is at the point where great disparities in economic power affect the expression of political power that the demand for economic democracy arises. And insofar as the logic of democracy is concerned a good case can be made for the claim that where political life is influenced by economic, legal, or even religious power political democracy by itself is *incomplete*. It is incomplete until its rationale of participation and uncoerced agreement, reached through the process of free discussion and criticism, has been extended to economic life as well, and until a true welfare

economy has been instituted which will reduce the great differences between economic classes and make them more nearly equal in economic power."[28]

But it is a contingent fact that the majority supports social and economic reforms. There is no contradiction in asserting that the majority is opposed to them, however unlikely it is that it would.

It would not always be possible to determine what the majority supports if part of the voting population were prohibited from voting. But this would not be so in the absence of the above welfare legislation.

"A legislative mistake in fixing rates, in taxation, in organizing administrative bureaus, in limiting hours or conditions of labor—can be corrected by a subsequent legislature representing the electorate that first authorized the law. But a law that changes the electorate or that denies it access to proper information cannot be reviewed by the same electorate. Legislation therefore that in any way affects the quantity or the quality of the body politic is in a peculiar position and must be subject to peculiar scrutiny."[29]

In which category does the right of free speech fall? Is it like voting rights or like welfare legislation? A minority in need of welfare legislation would be handicapped without welfare but could still exercise its voting rights, thus assuring majority rule. Likewise, a minority deprived of free speech, although severely handicapped, could still exercise its voting rights and thus make it possible for majority rule to continue.

Though majority rule with limited free speech would be better than minority rule, majority rule without restricted free speech would be better than majority rule with restricted free speech. But this is already to admit that majority rule with restricted freedom of speech is conceivable, and thus that majority rules does not logically imply unrestricted freedom of speech. Those who insist that unlimited free speech is logically part of majority rule because it is more desirable or effective are differing verbally about the meaning of majority rule, not about the desirability or effectiveness of unlimited free speech.

However, the mere right to vote cannot exhaust the total conditions required or logically implied by majority rule. Self-interest implies that disagreements will be reflected in the voting process and, in particular, majority and minority opinions. In order to arrive at majority and minority sentiment, at least two alternatives are required in any vote: to vote affirmatively or negatively for candidates, parties, programs, or issues.

Is is sufficient for majority rule to be able to vote merely affirmatively or negatively for only one candidate, party, etc., or is more than one required? It is clear that it is enough to vote either affirmatively or negatively in a referendum on only one issue, in order to ascertain the wishes of a majority. But if the voters are restricted to voting either affirmatively or negatively for only one candidate or party, and if the procedure of allowing that candidate or party which gets the most votes win is followed, the only party or candidate allowed to run will win even if a majority of the voters votes negatively. This would surely be inconsistent with majority rule and would in fact constitute minority rule. If, on the other hand, an affirmative vote of a majority is required to win, and the only candidate or party permitted to run fails to receive majority support, the elective office or position will not be filled. This too would be incompatible with majority rule, since the voters would not be represented by that office or position in government.

We see then that it is incompatible with majority rule to limit the voters to only one candidate or party. However, is restriction to only two or some other number compatible? It is possible for a majority to support a candidate or party not permitted to compete while at the same time fail to uphold the particular candidates or parties permitted to run. It does seem that the right to run for office is comparable to the right to vote, and that no restrictions be allowed in either case.

Even without curbs on the right to run for office, it is possible that no candidate or party will receive majority support. But, in this case, it could not be said that the majority was prevented from supporting its choice, whereas with restrictions there would always be the possibility of thwarting the will of the majority. Furthermore, without prohibitions on the right to run for office, and in the absence of any party or candidate receiving majority support, it is still possible to devise political means of forming a coalition of minorities representative of a majority of the voters and thus achieve some semblance of majority rule.

Another condition which is logically implied by majority rule is that the election results truly reflect the will of the majority. This implies that ballots are free and honest, that is, that they are conducted without coercion or fraud. Two conditions already cited as implied by majority rule, namely, the right to vote and the right to run for office, contribute to assuring free and honest elections. Voters and office seekers, because of self-interest are likely to attempt to insure that they are not deprived of winning as a result of elections that are not free and honest. However, are there any other procedures required to assure free and honest elections?

Since an open ballot exposes a voter to coercion for not voting contrary to his wishes, a secret ballot would surely be implied by free elections. Furthermore, since election results may be tabulated fraudulently, opportunities for rechecking and challenging figures must be made available to assure honest election returns. However, is it enough to permit only those who run for office the right to recheck or challenge the results?

Since coercion or collusion of candidates is possible, any procedures which reduce the possibility of fraud would seem mandatory. Hence it seems plausible not to restrict this right to a particular segment of the voting population, but rather to permit any voter the right to recheck or challenge the election results.

In discussing the necessity for free and honest elections, we have recognized the practical need of having the will of the voters reflected through their elected officials rather than by the voters themselves. No matter how frequently elections are held, and no matter how free and honest they may be, there is always the possibility of a gap or difference between the will of the majority and their representatives. As a result the will of the majority on some issues or on some occasions will be thwarted by their representatives, and to this extent majority rule will not be sustained. This requires providing machinery to permit all voters to initiate legislation and remove their elected officials through referendum and recall. These procedures are not intended as a substitute for but rather as a supplement to representative government. Majority rule is a matter of degree, a function of the number of decisions a majority is able to make, and, therefore, the right of the voters to referendum and recall increases the extent of majority rule.

FOOTNOTES

1. See Plato's *Republic,* for attack on democracy and defense of rule by the more able.
2. Henry Steele Commager, *Freedom and Order,* George Braziller, 1966, p. 6.
3. Herbert Marcuse, "Repressive Tolerance (Postscript 1968)," *A Critique of Pure Tolerance,* by R. P. Wolff, B. Moore, Jr., H. Marcuse, Beacon Paperback, 1969, pp. 120–121.
4. See *The Federalist Papers* for a rather careful analysis of the dangers of corruption as a basis for separation of powers and checks and balances.
5. Sidney Hook, *Reason, Social Myths and Democracy,* Humanities Press, 1950 reprint, p. 292.
6. *Ibid.,* p. 289.
7. See G. E. Moore's *Principia Ethica,* in which the so-called naturalistic fallacy is presented and attacked.
8. Henry Steele Commager, *Majority Rule and Minority Rights,* Oxford University Press 1943, p. 8.
9. *Ibid.,* p. 77.
10. Sidney Hook, *Political Power and Personal Freedom,* Collier Books, 1962, p. 48.
11. Henry Steele Commager, *Majority Rule and Minority Rights,* p. 72.

12. Martin Shapiro, *Freedom of Speech: The Supreme Court and Judicial Review,* Prentice Hall, 1966, p. 13.
13. John P. Roche, *Courts and Rights: The American Judiciary in Action,* second edition, Random House, 1966, p. 27.
14. Sidney Hook, *The Paradoxes of Freedom,* University of California Press, 1962, p. 89.
15. Leslie Lipson, *The Democratic Civilization,* Oxford University Press, 1964, p. 557.
16. Martin Shapiro, *op. cit.,* p. 102.
17. Sidney Hook, *The Paradoxes of Freedom, op. cit.,* p. 16.
18. Henry Steele Commager, *Majority Rule and Minority Rights,* pp. 58–59.
19. *Ibid.,* pp. 50–51.
20. Sidney Hook, *The Paradoxes of Freedom,* p. 93.
21. Henry Steele Commager, *Majority Rule and Minority Rights,* p. 47.
22. *Ibid.,* p. 56.
23. Martin Shapiro, *op. cit.,* p. 1.
24. John P. Roche, *op. cit.,* p. 26.
25. Henry Steele Commager, *Majority Rule and Minority Rights,* p. 20.
26. Henry Steele Commager, *Freedom and Order,* p. 14.
27. Sidney Hook, *Political Power and Personal Freedom,* p. 54.
28. *Ibid.,* pp. 55–56.
29. Henry Steele Commager, *Majority Rule and Minority Rights,* p. 67.

CHAPTER II

FREEDOM, EQUALITY, AND AUTHORITY

I. *The Individual and the State*

It is frequently said that democracy is committed to "freedom of the individual." The more limits imposed on the individual the less democratic is the society, and conversely, the less limits the more democratic. However, since limiting some individual's freedom may increase the freedom of others and conversely, it is not clear what it means to say that freedom of the individual is a measure of democracy. If we talk about freedom of the individual without specifying the individual and the kind of freedom we have in mind, we cannot get very far.

A clue to what freedom of the individual signifies may be found in the concept of majority rule, which we take to be an essential characteristic of democracy. A society governed by the will of the majority reflects the right of a majority to determine its laws, control its destiny, and choose its leaders.

"The common assumption is that with an electoral system based on equality of voting a majority of the representatives have been chosen by a majority of the voters, and hence, the majority rule in the legislature yields decisions as legitimate 'as if' they had been made directly by a majority of the voters, and indeed by a majority of all the adult citizens."[1] In this sense, freedom of the individual refers to the right of all to participate in the electoral processes, and the right of a majority to make the final decisions. Whether freedom of the individual exists depends on who controls the government, rather than whether an individual's freedom has been limited or extended by that government.

We have distinguished two uses of the phrase "freedom of the individual." One refers to the extent to which a person's freedom has been limited or broadened. The other refers

27

to the right of the majority to control its government. We have suggested that the latter sense can be plausibly derived from the claim that democracy is committed to freedom of the individual. Ambiguity in use may account for the contention that the more restrictions placed on an individual the more democracy is impaired.

Any country with majority rule is expected to prohibit certain actions. However, certain limits, such as restrictions on the right to vote, are incompatible with majority rule. Failure to distinguish between those limits which violate democratic principles and those which do not can lead to the conclusion that any restrictions are incompatible with a democratic society. These limits are incompatible with a democratic society, not because they restrict individual freedom, but because they prevent a majority from controlling its government.

However, some maintain democracy means more than mere majority rule, that it entails the protection of certain basic freedoms, such as free speech and free press, generally characterized as constitutional rights or part of the bill of rights. They hold that limits put on these rights are also incompatible with a democratic society and thus violate freedom of the individual. In this case, the concept of freedom of the individual has been broadened to include not only rights implicit in majority rule but also certain constitutional rights contained in a certain concept of a democratic society. But, again, these restrictions violate democratic principles, because they prohibit the exercise of constitutional rights, not because an individual's freedom has been limited. Thus, there are grounds for believing that freedom of the individual has been violated only where limits have been placed on such freedoms as the right to vote or constitutional rights. Apart from these, restrictions which have majority approval and constitutional sanction are compatible with a democratic society. In fact, certain restrictions are required to protect voting and constitutional rights and are thus essential to a democratic society.

Both advocates of majority rule and proponents of constitutional rights of minorities proclaim defense of individual freedom and democratic principles. This issue frequently reflects two varying concepts of democracy, namely, unqualified majority rule and constitutionally limited majority rule. It is clear that both positions require limiting some individuals' rights and extending the rights of others. Thus the problem is determining the individuals and freedom to be restricted. Supporters of unqualified majority rule may emphasize the fact of numbers, *i.e.*, a majority having priority over a minority, while supporters of qualified majority rule will stress the nature of the freedoms involved, *i.e.*, certain basic rights, such as free speech having priority over majority rule. Each contender, when defeated in any particular controversy, is likely to attack the government, since these disputes usually occur in the context of litigation involving some branch of authority. Thus a majority of individuals may claim that their individual rights are being violated by the government (usually judicial decisions) through excessive tolerance toward obscenity or crime. Or a minority of individuals may argue that their individual rights are being violated by highly restrictive court decisions against obscenity or the accused in criminal cases. They may see the issue in terms of freedom of the individual versus the government, though the issue may be one of evaluating alternative conflicting rights or freedoms. Neither side is likely to object to support by the government, which suggests that it is misleading to describe the conflict as one between individual freedom and the state.

It may be objected that there is a more fundamental question to be considered. It is embedded in the very concept of freedom, to which we attach such great importance, that holds that freedom deserves to be nourished and protected as an end in itself. It is not enough to protect those freedoms implicit in majority rule or those which make up our constitutional rights. It is essential to widen the range of freedoms humans are capable of experiencing. This constitutes one of the most important goals of a democratic society. This is, in part, what is meant by freedom of the individual.

Those who argue this way recognize that where freedoms conflict it is necessary to limit some freedoms in order to protect others of greater importance. But they express particular concern when the government extends its powers at the expense of individual citizens. They warn against the growing tendency of transferring power from individual citizens to the government, of letting the government do things formerly done by the people, of reducing the total area of freedom exercised by individuals and increasing the area of freedom in which government may function.

We can rely on voluntary agreement to guide the action of the state only so long as it is confined to spheres where agreement exists. But not only when the state undertakes direct control in fields where there is no such agreement is it bound to suppress individual freedom. We can unfortunately not indefinitely extend the sphere of common action and still leave the individual free in his own sphere. Once the communal sector, in which the state controls all the means, exceeds a certain proportion of the whole the effects of its actions dominate the whole system. Although the state controls directly the use of only a large part of the available resources, the effects of its decisions on the remaining part of the economic system become so great that indirectly it controls almost everything.[2]

Central to this position is the assumption that it is better for individuals to act on their own than to have the government act for them. "The fact is that, as our economy becomes more and more complex, it is increasingly difficult for a government planner sitting in Washington to take all the appropriate variables into account and make a correct decision."[3] But this is an empirical claim not substantiated in all matters, and particularly in dealing with problems beyond the capabilities of individuals on their own. One might just as well argue that a person ought to treat himself medically rather than employ the services of a doctor or a hospital, or that one ought to plant his own crops rather than rely on the produce of farmers, or that one ought to build a house with his own hands rather than hire a builder. Our need to rely on doctors, farmers, and builders is an acknowledgment that we cannot always act on our own; this recognition of dependency can be extended to local, state, and national governments. There are complex problems that neither local nor state authorities, let alone individuals, can adequately cope with, such as pollution, welfare, education, unemployment, inflation, housing, and so on. In light of the complexities of the contemporary age, is it wiser for individuals to act on their own rather than use the institutions of government?

There is another issue more significant than efficiency or capability, namely the extent to which citizens control their state. In a society where the people have little if any command of their government, those in authority can act arbitrarily without fear of reprisals at the ballot box. Under these circumstances, transferring power from individual citizens to the government increases the danger of abuse by the government. In such a society, it may be better for individuals to act on their own than have the government act for them. There is no elective pressure available to assure that the government will act for them.

However, in a society in which the people maintain control of their government, assignment of power from individuals to those in authority constitutes a delegation rather than a loss of power. The citizens are exercising their strength through the institutions of government instead of directly. No doubt the following is an exaggeration:

"We should keep in mind that whenever government exercises authority in America, it is the American people who exercise that authority."[4]

However, as long as the people are able to control the use

of this power, and to reverse the transfer of power if they so choose, they have not surrendered their freedom.

"But the coming of democracy has converted the state from the agent of a privileged few to the agent of the whole. In such a state, properly actualized, the government is the people's own; it is their instrument, not their master. As such, it can provide men with those conditions that make freedom both possible and meaningful, and that they cannot otherwise attain by themselves, such as education and adequate medical care."[5]

Though the distinction between undemocratic and democratic societies is crucial, countries do not fall neatly into these two categories. Even the most democratic nations fall short of being under complete control of the people; thus, transfer of power to government runs some risk of abuse. But there is an alternative risk of abuse by individuals or institutions other than government.

"But controls derive too from sources other than the state. They are imposed by private powers no less than by political governments, thus producing a paradoxical situation in which political restraints, by curbing nonpolitical restraints, may assure freedom to those who would otherwise be controlled by private powers."[6] This is even true in undemocratic societies. Where there are advantages in using the institutions of government, it makes more sense to remove defects in the democratic processes rather than oppose transfer of power to the government.

It is clear that in any society where majority rule prevails, a minority of individuals will be opposed to some decisions which limit that minority. They may express concern that freedom of the individual is being violated, that the people are losing their freedom, or that the government is increasing its power at the expense of its citizens. This may mislead us into thinking that a majority of the people are losing their freedom though only a minority are; that a majority of the people are opposed to these decisions though only a minority are; that these decisions run counter to the interests of a majority of all of the people though it may run counter to the interests of a minority and be in the interests of a majority. If these decisions reflect majority will, then they represent the freedom of a majority even if at the expense of the freedom of a minority.

Thus, if the power to fix rates is transferred from a utility to the government, then the majority exercises the right to fix utility rates at the expense of the utility. If the utility complains that freedom of the individual is being violated, it may mean that freedom of a minority is begin restricted. If it is wrong to limit the right of a minority to fix rates, is it not also wrong to limit the right of the majority to fix rates?

The objection that compulsion of any individual or minority is inherently wrong or incompatible with individual freedom or democracy raises the question of what alternatives are available short of anarchism, since it is virtually impossible to obtain unanimity on most issues. In the absence of unanimity, either the minority or the majority will have to be coerced since refusal to coerce a minority to accept the will of the majority will constitute coercion of majority will.

"Principles must take cognizance of facts, and the facts show that, when men are consulted about their preferences, they normally subdivide into many groups. If, however, the choices are reduced to two alternatives, there will be a majority facing a minority. Government, therefore, must be conducted by one or other of these. Since democracy cannot concede the right of the few to prevail over the many the only possibility that remains is majority rule."[7] If coercion of a minority is incompatible with individual freedom, coercion of a majority is even more so.

Valid objections can be raised to curtailing the freedom of a minority or transferring its power to government. It could result in less efficiency, less incentive, more abuse, or more harm to society.

"Belief in what is sometimes called taking industry out of private hands is naive until it is shown that the new private —or personal—hands to which it is confided are so controlled that they are reasonably sure to work in behalf of public ends."[8] Transfer or restriction of power is neither inherently good nor bad, and cannot be defended or condemned in the abstract. It needs to be evaluated in light of experience and evidence, on the basis of projected consequences for each particular case. It will not do, however, to raise the cry that this is necessarily incompatible with freedom of the individual or a democratic society.

What about limits placed on a majority or power transferred from a majority to the government, e.g., subjecting a majority of the citizens to an income tax? Here also the power to dispose of the revenue is controlled by the majority of citizens to the extent that they exercise dominion over the government, notwithstanding the fact that they cannot use the money in their private capacity or on an individual basis. It is more accurate to say that they have chosen not to spend the money individually rather than that they cannot, since they could have if they had so desired. They could have disapproved of the tax, and they can eliminate it. It is even misleading to characterize it as a limit on the majority or a transfer of power from the majority to the government. This obscures the fact that this is a self-limiting act, and that this power has not really been given or taken away, but is still retained by the majority through control over those in authority. No one would maintain that I am not free to use my money if I choose not to spend it. No one would maintain that I do not have the power to use my money if I authorize an agent to spend it for me and I retain control over how he disposes of it.

"If I agree, freely and uncoerced, to a set of principles, institutions, and procedures, then anything done in conformity with them is authoritative for me because authorized by me. By this reasoning, if I was consulted and have consented, I am the author of the acts of which the public official is the agent. Indeed, my authorship is his authority. Thus when I obey the state, I do not bow to an external will, but express my own."[9]

Another important consideration is the use by the government of its power. "The native canniness of the individual is not equal to the task of judging the safety of the drugs he buys or the planes he rides in. He must be served by regulatory agencies. Our great national parks and forests provide benefits that could not be had through individual action. Our postal system performs a service that can only be done nationally."[10] If it spends the taxes collected to build hospitals, schools, or roads, then the freedom or power of its citizens has been enlarged in being able to utilize these facilities. If it fixes utility rates in a reasonable way then it may protect the consumer's freedom from being abused by exorbitant rates. The government's power may be employed to protect and enlarge more of its citizens' freedoms than it limits. In a democratic society the majority not only has the right to control and direct the power of government, but to use this right to enlarge the freedoms of all.

II. *Equality and Discrimination*

We are told that equality is a hallmark of a democratic society, something to be nourished, protected, and defended. "Men being, as has been said, by nature all free, equal, and independent, no one can be put out of this estate and subjected to the political power of another without his own consent. The only way whereby any one divests himself of his natural liberty and puts on the bonds of civil society is by agreeing with other men to join and unite into a community for their comfortable, safe, and peaceable living one amongst another, in a secure enjoyment of their properties and a greater security against any that are not of it."[11]

To the extent that inequalities exist, we have failed to achieve one of the most cherished ideals of democracy. A good deal of ink and blood has been spilled, energy exerted, and money spent in the effort to remove inequalities of different minority groups. The issues of racial, religious, and ethnic discrimination have become daily concerns of practically everyone.

Men are not equal in native ability, education, experience,

or wealth. But this would be true even if all discrimination were eliminated. Thus, it is not at all clear what is meant by saying that equality is desirable. Suppose everyone were made equal in wealth. Since people vary in how much they spend and save, they would eventually end up being unequal in wealth. Assume everyone were given equal access to education and experience. Since they differ in the kinds of education and experience they choose to pursue, they would eventually end up with different kinds of knowledge and experience. Some individuals would be better equipped in certain fields than others. Inequalities would exist in knowledge and experience.

"Suppose one could assume a hypothetical community where all individuals began the race of life with the same chance, where family connections, parental influence, and wealth, had no bearing on one's education and later advancement, and where all freedoms were perfectly equalized. In such an imaginary society, the different abilities of the individual would still assert themselves. Those with better minds, stronger bodies, more forceful personalities, would show their superiority and thrust ahead."[12] Suppose everyone were equal in native ability. Since they would use their abilities in diverse ways by engaging in different pursuits, they would turn out unequal in interests, knowledge, training, experience, and wealth. We are confronted with the conclusion that the attainment of equality would ultimately result in inequality. If equality is desirable so is inequality.

It may be said that one ought not to confuse being different with being unequal or being equal with being the same. If two individuals are given equal access to education, they are equal even though they end up with different educational backgrounds. But equality cannot be spoken of in the abstract; it must be specified with respect to what characteristic two individuals are equal or unequal. Thus, the two individuals may have been equal with respect to admission to school. But if one has become a doctor and the other a lawyer, then they are unequal with respect to their particular qualifications, the doctor being superior with respect to medical training, the lawyer being superior with respect to legal training, and so on. If one individual lacks a particular characteristic another one possesses, then they are unequal (not the same) with respect to that characteristic. Of course absence of one particular characteristic may be compensated for by the presence of another, which accounts in part for our support of equal access to education, for example, without which there would not even be this compensation. Thus, though certain equalities result in other inequalities, this is preferable to causing even more inequalities because of the absence of compensating inequalities.

It will be said that all that is meant by equality is the absence of discrimination. The only kind of equality that is objectionable is caused by discrimination, which consists of treating people unequally on unjust grounds.

"The doctrine of equality never meant what some of its critics supposed it to mean. It never asserted equality of natural gifts. It was a moral, a political and legal principle, not a psychological one."[13] Treating people unequally on just grounds is not discrimination. That inequalities exist or that people are treated unequally is not sufficient grounds for holding that the inequalities are undesirable. In fact, treating people equally may be undesirable where there are just grounds for treating them differently.

"The man who presses for 'equality of opportunity' is urging that certain factors, like wealth, which have hitherto determined the extent of an individual's opportunities, should be neutralized. But he may very well be urging at the same time discrimination according to other criteria. Because in the mouth of the egalitarian 'equality' is a term of approval, he is bound to distinguish between differences in treatment that are reasonable, and therefore compatible with 'equality,' and those that are not, and are thus 'inequalities.' "[14] There is no more basis for treating people equally than unequally unless there are valid reasons for so treating them.

What kinds of inequality are unjustified and what kinds

of equality are unjustified? Treating individuals unequally on discriminatory grounds is unjustified. But this does not get us very far since discriminatory grounds are unjustified grounds. Why do we maintain that treating individuals unequally on the grounds of race, color, or creed is unjustified and thus discriminatory? We believe that these considerations are not relevant to a person's ability to perform a job or obtain an education. Is there reason for treating people equally in the absence of reasons for treating them unequally? Should we treat everyone alike unless there are grounds not to? It may seem difficult to find reasons for equal treatment independent of the fact that there are no valid reasons for unequal treatment. Historically, unequal treatment in the absence of valid reasons for unequal treatment has been interpreted as unequal treatment for invalid reasons, i.e., on discriminatory grounds. In light of reasons given that are invalid, e.g., race, color, and creed, and the harmful consequences, the absence of valid reasons for unequal treatment constitutes sufficient grounds for equal treatment. But treating people equally regardless of ability, education, or experience may be unjustified, since these factors may affect a person's ability to perform a job or pursue an education. "It is not equality of result that justice demands, but equality of opportunity and fairplay: given these, it is the significant measurement of unequal merit that is just."[15] Thus merit constitutes one criterion for determining whether individuals are to be treated equally or unequally.

But the criterion of merit does not always hold. Minorities have been deprived of positions or education because of race, color, or creed. It is felt that some compensation is required for having treated them unequally in the past.

"And we do more than treat everyone as if they started on an equal footing: we attempt to compensate for some personal disadvantages, as well as giving preferential treatment to special talents. We have schools for disabled, blind, and deaf children, and we spend far more per head on them than we do on the average child. If this is not accounted 'inequality of opportunity,' it is because the discrimination is felt to be justified."[16] Two individuals may be equally capable of performing a certain job. The criterion of merit implies that both individuals shall be given equal opportunity to obtain that job. Suppose one of these persons belongs to a minority group which has been deprived of obtaining similar jobs in the past. It is felt that in order to make up for inequities, members of the minority group should receive preferential treatment in acquiring the position. This implies that the two individuals shall be treated unequally even though they are equally competent to perform the job.

Similar considerations apply to one deprived of education and experience because of discrimination. "Negroes do suffer a special handicap. But a great deal must be attributed to the low level of educational qualification among Negroes, reflecting not discrimination, *per se*, by the industrial system but prior disadvantage in schools and environment."[17] He may be given equal if not preferred consideration in obtaining a job, even if less capable than another individual with superior education and experience. Two individuals might be treated equally even though they are not equally capable.

It may be argued that the above examples reflect an attempt to promote equality by reducing or eliminating the effects of past discrimination. It would be measuring equality and discrimination statistically, in terms of groups rather than individuals. But it would not be judging each individual on a basis of ability. The person who did not get the job could claim that he was not treated without regard to race, color or creed. He might very well feel that he was discriminated against. Granted that it would differ in intention from the usual variety of discrimination, it would still be a departure from the principle that an individual should be judged on the basis of ability, regardless of race, color, or creed. It would reflect a paradoxical situation in which attainment of equality for minority groups results in inequality for certain individuals.

"From 1967 onward, open and covert conflict, not consensus, will dominate the relationships between Negro and White America, as well as the relationships between Negroes and Negroes, in the struggle for equal rights, opportunities, and progress. For if Negroes in the slum ghettos are to achieve genuine progress it will mean that whites must deliberately divest themselves of certain political, social, and economic advantages for redistribution among black have-nots."[18]

How can we resolve the conflict between group equality and individual equality, or between group discrimination and individual discrimination? Even those who support compensating minorities for past discrimination would recognize that it is not always feasible to give them the job. Suppose the job required medical knowledge and training and necessitated making decisions involving the health and even lives of individuals. The injustices resulting from lack of knowledge and experience would outweigh the injustices resulting from past discrimination.

How would the conflict be resolved if the job did not involve anything as vital as the health or lives of humans? Suppose someone belonging to a minority group had been prevented from obtaining that kind of position as a consequence of past bias. It would seem equitable to give him preference over an individual who had not been subject to discrimination, even if they are equally capable. But the fact that a minority group has been discriminated against in a certain field does not imply that every member of that group has been so treated. It may be true that some members of that group have been prevented from obtaining that kind of job. Suppose the individual under consideration has not been so treated. Why should he receive preferred treatment merely because he belongs to a group containing members who have been discriminated against? In this case, the criterion of ability seems to be the more feasible approach.

Of course, minorities have been discriminated against in many respects; a member of that minority might be given preferred treatment in this particular case, even though he suffered in an entirely different respect. But his rival for the job may have also suffered other forms of discrimination or injustices stemming from sources other than racial discrimination (poverty, ignorance, illness, cruel or no parents). The process of attempting to equalize or reduce inequities can become rather complicated.

Sharp controversy has arisen recently in the United States over a Selective Service system providing for deferments and exemptions incompatible with treating people equally. Even the strongest proponents of equality recognize the need for exempting those who fail to meet minimum mental and physical standards from military service. But apart from this qualification conflict has been aroused between the principle of equality and educational deferments and exemptions. The need for medical doctors, scientists, teachers, etc., for both civilian and military purposes may compel putting aside the principle of equality. In the absence of serious shortages of specialized skills, training, and education, it may be satisfactory to draft individuals on a "random" basis which approximates the ideal of equality of military obligation. But even among those called to serve, a variety of needs and talents requires unequal treatment including unequal risks involving life and death itself. One is not likely to object to subjecting a medical doctor to less risk on the battlefield than an unskilled soldier if this increases the number of lives saved as a consequence of a doctor's medical knowledge and skill. Even if educational deferments were eliminated, different abilities and cultural backgrounds would result in unequal benefits, including sending some draftees to colleges under military auspices for special training to serve the needs of the armed forces. Similar consequences would ensue if universal military training were adopted for the purpose of equalizing the obligation of all to serve the country in some capacity. Thus, the principle of equality does not always deserve priority over other criteria, such as need, ability, experience, or knowledge.

We have seen that treating individuals equally is not always desirable. Some would suggest that recognition and reward of individual effort and individual differences also characterize a democratic society. "On the one hand democracy is the form of society which rewards winners regardless of origin. On the other hand it is the form of society which gives losers the widest latitude in rewriting the rules of the contest. No one who has not thought long and hard about these paradoxical facts is in a position to understand the tug of war between equality and excellence in a democracy."[19] Yet we believe that equality is somehow bound up with a democratic society. In what way is this so? A democratic society is characterized by consent of the governed as reflected by majority rule. This implies political equality in choosing our representatives and making our laws. Equal voting rights are basic to a democratic society.

"(a) Every adult should have the vote—the familiar device of the universal adult suffrage. Popular control defines the 'people' as all adult citizens, although there are of course minor differences in the definitions of an 'adult.'

"(b) One person should have one vote—that is, there should be no plural voting.

"(c) Each vote should count equally—that is, votes are not weighed in any way."[20]

But shall everybody be permitted to vote or run for office? Even advocates of universal suffrage grant that minimum qualifications should be stipulated for the right to vote or hold office, such as age, residence, and literacy requirements. Complete equality of all citizens is not considered necessary for political equality in a democratic society. But apart from minimum qualifications, political equality is believed to be inherent in a democracy. Without political equality we cannot have majority rule and without majority rule we cannot have a democratic society. Political equality presupposes that all qualified citizens shall have an equal right to vote and run for office. This implies that no qualified citizen shall be disenfranchised. No citizen's vote shall have a greater weight than another citizen's vote. Exclusion from voting or running for office on the grounds of race, color, or creed is forbidden.

But does majority rule or democracy also prohibit discrimination in matters other than voting or running for office? Suppose a majority approves of the right to hire or sell property to whomever one wishes. This implies the right to discriminate in hiring or selling property. Barring a majority from approving of this right would limit democracy by interfering with the will of the majority. We have a conflict between majority rule and equality in obtaining a job or buying property. Permitting discrimination would violate the economic rights of a minority. But preventing discrimination would violate the political rights of a majority. We find that consent of the governed may result in inequality. We grant that economic inequality resulting from discrimination is undesirable. But so is thwarting majority rule.

On the other hand a majority may endorse outlawing discrimination in employment or buying property. There are those who would object to this on the grounds that it violates the right to hire or sell property to whomever one wishes. But preventing a majority from outlawing discrimination would also be incompatible with majority rule.

Democracy permits one to disagree with the majority and try to change its mind. Which is more important, the right to discriminate or the right not to be discriminated against? Which should we attempt to persuade the majority to accept? It will be argued that the issue is not the right of discrimination but the right to hire or sell property to whomever one wishes. Ownership of a business or property implies the right to determine how it shall be run or disposed of. This does not mean that one will discriminate, for some who support this right are opposed to discrimination. There are all kinds of reasons for hiring or selling property to certain individuals, having nothing to do with discrimination. Restrictions on this right will in effect strip ownership of meaning. Assume for the moment that this is the correct interpretation of the issue. Which is more essential, the right to control one's business or property, or the right to prevent discrimination? One approach is to ask which right is of greater benefit to society? Or which right, if taken away, will result in greater harm to society?

But there is something wrong with putting the issue this

way. Preventing discrimination does not remove completely command of one's business or property. It restricts that right in only one respect, namely, the right to discriminate. It removes only one among a variety of reasons for not hiring or selling property to certain individuals. One may still refuse to hire on a basis of market conditions or ability to perform the job. One may still refuse to sell property on the basis of price offered or ability to meet mortgage payments. Apart from the right to discriminate one still has control over one's business or property.

Stated more correctly, the issue is the right to discriminate versus the right to prohibit discrimination. Which right is of greater benefit to society? We must distinguish between different kinds of bias. What may be appropriate for discrimination in hiring or selling property may not be so in personal associations or marriage. There are even variations in each of these categories. Thus, hiring a domestic servant or tutor may not have the same consequences as hiring a clerk or bricklayer. Generally speaking, a good case can be made against discrimination in employment. Though prohibiting prejudice in hiring might be unpalatable for those who wish to discriminate, permitting discrimination would seem in most cases to have more harmful psychological, social, and economic consequences. Similar considerations apply to prejudice in housing, education, and public accommodations. Outlawing discrimination in close personal relationships may be self-defeating. Hiring a personal valet is an example of this kind. This is comparable to preventing bias in friendship or marriage. We are not suggesting that discrimination is justified even in close personal relationships. But there are some situations in which legal restrictions against discrimination will not succeed.

One ought not to take an "all" or "nothing" view of whether morality can be legislated. One can hope to legislate effectively against certain kinds of behavior, such as discrimination in public housing, restaurants, schools, public accommodations, even if individuals remain biased internally. On the other hand, one cannot expect to legislate successfully against discrimination in marriage or friendship for the very relationships involved preclude coercion in order to succeed.

We have not considered constitutional questions arising from discrimination. It is open to anyone to approve of constitutional changes in support of their views on discrimination. We have been concerned with the justification of these beliefs. Even if the Constitution prohibits or permits certain kinds of discrimination, it does not settle the question of desirability. One who appeals to the Constitution in support of or in opposition to certain kinds of discrimination may be relying on the view that obeying the constitution is justified. But whether discrimination is desirable is another matter.

III. *Democracy in the University*

The ivory tower, once popularly characterized as a citadel of learning, has been recently undergoing internal convulsions. There is increasing clamor to transform universities into democratic institutions or our commitment to a free society will be exposed as inconsistent, hypocritical, and self-serving. Some call for dividing authority equally among students, faculty, and administration, or even on the basis of one man one vote. Apparently this line of reasoning requires wider distribution of power, including the right of students to make decisions formerly restricted to faculty.

Perhaps, in the same spirit, the outside community should be invited into areas previously regarded as university domain. The faculty is only a minority of the university, but the university is even a smaller minority of society. No doubt this suggestion would evoke criticism, not only from the academic halls but from major community spokesmen who would consider it an abdication of academic responsibility. But isn't opposition to outside involvement in higher education a violation of the democratic principle of consent of the governed?

Some will deny that barring the community from campus affairs is undemocratic as long as all university members participate in educational decisions. But if being democratic merely requires equal power for those within specific boundaries, with no role for outsiders, the same holds for drawing boundaries around faculty and excluding outsiders from faculty affairs. If it is not undemocratic for the university not to share power with the community, it is not undemocratic for the faculty not to share power with the students.

If the primary interest and concern of academic members are given as grounds for barring the community from campus decisions, similar grounds can be suggested for excluding students from faculty decisions. Thus, the total academic community utilizes and consequently has a greater concern for adequate eating, lighting, and recreational facilities on the campus than the public; the faculty are more directly involved in and thus have greater concern for the quality of publications, research, and teaching than the students. In the former case, the university should make the decisions, in the latter, the faculty. That faculty decisions affect students is of course true, but so do university decisions affect the community. Thus, faculty decisions concerning publications, research, and teaching affect students; likewise university decisions concerning eating, lighting, and recreational facilities affect the community (so do, incidentally, the faculty decisions on publication research and teaching). If student concern with faculty decisions justifies sharing power with the faculty, then community concern with university decisions justifies sharing power with the university. Granted that the concern of the community and the university differ in degree and kind, the same can be said for the faculty and students. Ironically, if the community were directly involved in university decisions, it would probably support removing or banning those very forces on campus most vociferous about the democratic right of students to be directly involved in university decisions. It is not being suggested that the community be directly involved in university decisions, but rather that similar considerations apply to the direct involvement of students in faculty decisions.

It is true that the community plays an indirect role in

education, through control of funds, election of political representatives who choose boards of trustees, and so on. But members of the academic community (including students) also participate in this role since they are also members of the community at large. (Students' lack of voting rights in society requires political reform, not special privileges in education.) The community is not expected to participate directly in educational decisions such as, admissions, curriculum content, faculty hiring, firing, and promotion, and degree requirements. If this is compatible with democracy, so is the exclusion of students from faculty decisions. If indirect involvement of the community is a necessary condition of democracy, then everyone (including students) does or should participate through the political process.

There are those who draw a parallel between universities and local governments. Generally, each local government possesses autonomy reflecting a boundary within which its citizens are entitled to an equal voice. Since the university is also granted autonomy, it is inferred that its members are also entitled to an equal voice. Note that they are not granted autonomy for identical reasons. The local states' independence reflects geographical interests and political functions, while educational independence serves the goals of academic freedom and the acquisition of knowledge and truth. Furthermore, this line of reasoning reflects the fallacy of argument from analogy which consists of concluding that two things are similar in certain respects because they are similar in other respects. If citizens are obligated to pay taxes to their local governments, are members of the academic community also obligated to pay taxes to their university? Since the university awards degrees, shall the governments do the same? Since the government provides jails, shall the university do likewise?

Equality in a political system does not automatically sanctify its use in another institution; it requires independent grounds, taking into account the function of that institution.

"How should I be greeted if I demanded a place on next

year's All-American football team because I am a citizen and therefore the equal of any candidate for a place? Does the enlisted man get his turn at playing commander of the forces in the field?"[21] If citizens deserve equal power in controlling a state government, does it entail equal power in practicing medicine, engineering, or running an educational institution?

"The influence of the democratic ideal on collegiate opportunity can never imply equality of standing, but only equality of *standard.*"[22] One can make a case for democracy within Alabama. But one ought not confuse a political subdivision of society (Alabama) which serves a political function, with universities or hospitals which serve different functions.

Some believe that what is true of a whole must also be true of its parts, that if democracy is justified in society as a whole, it is also true for any part, or institution of society. This smacks of the "fallacy of division," illustrated by the belief that if a whole baseball team is two years old, each member of the team must also be two years old. If majority rule is appropriate for a nation, it is not necessarily so for a hospital, bank, army, prison, or university in that nation.

Some decisions of a minimal or secondary importance could and should be and are in fact made by all members of these institutions. But the basic decisions, those requiring special knowledge, training and experience (including the very question of what is a minimal or minor decision) are in a different category. Would it be reasonable for patients to vote on how a hospital is to be run, medication administered, or surgery performed? Should bank tellers or depositors decide how a bank is to be run or what investments are desirable? Shall the private plan military campaign strategy or supervise espionage activities? Ought the prisoners to supervise the running of a prison? Or would competence in making decisions be a more sound guide?

The function and goals of the university are not confined to the needs and interests of students; the faculty, administration, and, indeed, society, also have needs no less important. But even if students were the exclusive concern of the campus, it would not sustain the view that they are qualified to cope with these needs. One can make as good a case that patients are the *raison d'être* for hospitals as one can that students are the *raison d'être* for universities. Shall patients operate hospitals because they constitute the main purpose of hospitals?

Undoubtedly, students have interests, needs, knowledge, and information relevant to the function of schools, just as patients have relevant to the function of doctors and hospitals; these should be sought and provided for. But how to satisfy the needs and interests, how to utilize the knowledge and information is a matter of competence; there is as little reason to believe that students are capable of fulfilling these functions as there is that patients are.

Of course, students, like any other group, have varying degrees of knowledge and experience; a few, particularly at higher levels of education (graduate school) are already teaching and doing research. But this means that they have already begun to qualify as teachers and scholars and are no longer merely students. Their role in decision making reflects the criterion of competence, not democracy. Students not qualified to teach, make innumerable decisions commensurate with their proficiency: choice of major field, area of specialization within major field and electives, choice of teachers (the general practice of "shopping around" for courses), selection of extracurricular activities (religious, political, and social), student government and newspapers, and so on. But their right to make these decisions reflects the principle of competence, which qualifies them as students and distinguishes them from the community at large.

If varying competence of the academic and nonacademic world differentiates their role in higher education, the same holds for different members of the academic community. Some suggest that students have proficiency comparable to the faculty which distinguishes them (students) from the nonacademic sector. Some students may be more capable than some people off campus, but how they compare with faculty or anyone else obviously depends on the individual and the specific area of knowledge.

It seems clear that "The faculty of a university is the only body competent to determine what general knowledge and what specialized education are necessary for a continuation of professional knowledge and professional skill."[23] There are varieties of background among faculty which qualify them for different kinds of decisions. Normally, no one expects the physics teacher to determine the sociology curriculum; indeed, the student majoring in sociology is ostensibly better equipped, though the sociology teacher would probably be the most proficient.

The question of curriculum control encompasses a variety of problems requiring different kinds of knowledge and experience: determining the courses required to fulfill a major field; deciding the programs necessary to satisfy degree requirements; planning budgets which affect the size, quality, and variety of classes, and so on. Many faculty members lack the knowledge and experience essential for coping with certain curriculum problems, particularly budget matters. Students are precluded from determining curriculum, not only because they lack proficiency, but because of a conflict of interest between meeting and setting educational requirements.

The temptation is too great to allow those about to meet qualifying standards to have a voice in determining them. It is not common to find students calling for more requirements, more grades, more examinations, higher standards— rather, the contrary. Even the call for "better" teaching frequently reflects the desire for "easier" teachers and "better" grades.

There are administrators and faculty who overemphasize research and disregard the needs of students in the classroom. "Research worth having can only be hoped for, not commanded; yet in the best schools teaching is deemed inferior to it and a nuisance."[24] On the other hand "The teaching of graduate students is so closely tied to research that if research is improved, graduate instruction is almost bound to be improved also."[25]

The problem of determining and balancing good teaching and research is difficult enough for faculty; to compound it by bringing into the decision making process those even less qualified to judge is to encourage inferior judgments. It is clear that students are not in a position to evaluate the scholarly work of the teacher. It is less clear that this applies to his quality as a good teacher. It is frequently assumed that, since students have direct contact with teachers in the classroom, they are in a specially privileged position to judge the teacher as teacher. What can they judge? They can tell whether he is interesting, amusing, kind, witty, friendly, clear, stimulating, late, absent, and so on. Probably the teacher's own colleagues, wife, children, relatives, and friends can make most of these types of judgment. But how significant are these for good teaching? Does the teacher know his subject well, is he up-to-date, is his presentation fair, balanced, comprehensive, is he doing research and what kind in the area he is teaching? Aren't these the significant kinds of considerations for good teaching? Are the students in a position to pass judgments in these matters?

There are teachers who are unsympathetic, boring, arbitrary, cruel, incompetent, oppressive, and deserving of dismissal. There should be machinery (including right of appeal) available to deal with these problems. But granting students authority to hire, fire, and promote faculty who in turn will pass on students may have unpleasant consequences.

There is enough truth in the following statement to make one pause: "Overhear a group of average students talking about their teachers and you will find the near majority agreed on warning the rest: 'Don't take *his* course: he tries to make you think.' "[26] Students not only lack competence in choosing faculty but suffer from a conflict of interest with faculty which could lead to collusion, intimidation, and even blackmail. Similar considerations apply to faculty selecting administrators and boards of trustees. Procedures of these kinds may lead to a dilution of the quality of decisions, the hiring and promotion of the less able, loss of the more capable, and deterioration of administrative, teaching, and learning standards.

It must be granted that having faculty chosen by their own peers also involves a conflict of interest, since they are subject to rivalry and jealousy in promotions, merit increases, publications, and so on. Of course, any evaluation involves this to some extent. It is difficult to determine which conflict causes greater risk or harm. The dangers of abuse can be handled through appeals machinery to higher levels of authority, including administration and ultimately the political machinery, including the judicial and legislative processes. All of these are available to students and faculty. But the fundamental question of qualifications to judge makes all the difference in the world.

That the most capable are not always successful or correct does not warrant disregarding degrees of competence. The following attitude is reflected in some quarters: "Often enough students are wrong in their opinions about academic life and educational policy, but then so too are the rest of us; and a supply of fresh mistakes might be invigorating."[27] However, fallibility implies that one is not always correct, not that everyone is equally correct; it does not deny that some judgments are more reliable, more probable, more sound than others, merely that no judgment is completely certain. One might as well permit laymen to operate because surgeons are fallible. Or perhaps we ought to invite nonacademic citizens to hire faculty and formulate curricula. Academic members convinced that injustices are occurring in the name of competence need remember that opportunities are available for obtaining credentials required for making decisions, that many administrators were once faculty members and all faculty members were once students.

Where deficient, machinery is needed to channel complaints of students or faculty. As individuals and in groups, they can engage in social and political activities on and off the campus, to persuade, argue, debate, complain, propagandize, and petition for academic and other reforms. But should they expect more privileges than others to make decisions involving special knowledge and training?

There are differences concerning the purpose of a university. "The ideal of the advancement and transmission of knowledge in the universities has met another strong ideal native in America, the assumption that educational institutions should be useful to the society."[28]

But it seems reasonable not to restrict the functions of a university, not to be forced to choose between the intellectual and the social needs. "Today the seemingly antagonistic traditions of separateness and involvement exist side by side in our greatest universities. At the heart of any great American university there is the kind of insulation from the market place that permits reflective and creative thought. At the same time in other parts of the university, there is extensive interaction with the rest of the society."[29]

It is somewhat misleading to separate the purely scholarly function from the social one, since theoretical knowledge is indirectly beneficial to the public. But the distinction is useful in pointing out the differences between short-run or immediate community needs and long-run ones. The university may cater to the latter in developing tastes and interests of lasting intellectual value, in encouraging scientific and artistic innovations and discoveries which require longer periods of time to blossom and which may have little practical value even in the long run. It is understandable that the public is more skeptical about these abstract considerations than about more mundane and immediately practical functions. It is also understandable that reformers or critics feel that the university should play a greater role in dealing with our social and economic problems, poverty, the ghetto, education, urban decay, housing and so on. It is to be expected that given limited resources, conflicts will arise over its allocation between the theoretical and practical needs, the short-run and long-run goals, the requirements of the ghetto, the professions, and industry. Differences over the function of a university have aggravated the struggle over decision making, each faction hoping it will be able to fashion the university in its own image. Ironically, one's view of the function of a university may not be in accord with those one thinks should run it.

Ironically also, a struggle over allocation of funds may result in defeat for all if the ceiling on total resources is kept tight or reduced. It should be kept in mind that we may insist on more resources to ease the problem of allocation. It must also be conceded that the university is more uniquely equipped to deal with the long run, theoretical questions than other institutions. Put another way, other institutions, particularly the government and its agencies, are available to cope with the immediate social and economic problems.

Whether the function of a university is scholarship or teaching or public service or anything else, it is desirable that the most capable decide how it is to be fulfilled, though ultimately answerable to the citizenry. In this way, the principles of competence and democracy are satisfied. One hopes society can be persuaded for its own good not to intervene directly in university affairs, that education, like medicine or engineering, operates most effectively when run by the best qualified. Will the public look favorably at appeals for non-intervention and economic aid if they find that the university itself does not adhere to the principle of competence?

Recently state and federal legislation have been passed calling for restriction of funds and intervention in higher education. This is partly a reaction against concessions to student power and weakening of educational standards. The academic community, which might normally be expected to be united for academic independence and maximum financial aid from all source, is split; many faculty members are demoralized, disillusioned, bitter, and have even supported cutting funds and outside intervention. A few have begun to look for institutions holding the line against deterioration of standards. All of this must be taken into account by critics of competence concerned with the future of education.

Some believe that talk of competence reflects an illusion

that the university is committed to the ideals of truth and knowledge.

"The growing involvement of the Western university as the research arm of the governing elite has, for example, led some critics to view it as a 'tool' of the establishment."[30] They see it as a tool of those who wield power in society, a source of training and indoctrination in maintaining the *status quo* and the Establishment. To them, the university is just another institution in society constituting a battleground in the struggle for power between the few on top and those at the bottom whom they dominate and control. The call for greater student participation in running the university is considered an extension of the fight of the poor, the minorities, and the have-nots for power in society as a whole.

"New-left theorists regard issues in university reform as matters around which larger masses of students may be 'radicalized' or 'politicized' toward eventual reform of other social institutions."[31] They regard education as a fertile base for winning adherents among those not yet captured by the vested interests in industry and government. It is part of what is meant by those who wish to politicize or radicalize the universities.

Ironically, this anti-Establishment view is shared by some of the most orthodox political forces who have looked upon the intellectual rhetoric of "academic freedom" and "open campus" as naïveté at best, and a subversive plot at worst.

"There are those in the population, even among the alumni and the boards of trustees of some universities, who resent the fact that the university is a haven for dissent and for the free examination of assumptions and practices. They often strive to diminish this fundamental role of a university. They seem to imagine that the chief role of the university is to endorse the status quo."[32]

These ultraconservative segments of society conceive of education as a tool for transmitting traditional values and mores, a form of indoctrination in the American Way of Life. There is evidence that the *status quo* has substantial support among the students on campus. "In the United States today, the largest campus political groups are the Young Democrats and Young Republicans, which have a total combined membership of under 250,000 members, as contrasted to 7,000 members of the new-left Students for a Democratic Society (SDS). A recent (1967) U.S. survey of American college students reports that a plurality favors the Republicans for the 1968 Presidential Election. Four national surveys conducted during 1965 and 1966 found that from two thirds to three quarters of American students support the Vietnamese war."[33]

Thus, in the attempt to politicize and radicalize the universities, the radicals may discover that they have helped open the door to those traditional forces who are far more powerful, politically and financially, in any final showdown. Since the radicals have a greater hearing on campus under the "illusion" of academic freedom than elsewhere, the destruction of this illusion would constitute a cutting of their own throats.

Critics must admit that the university has constituted a greater base for dissent that any other institution. This is one reason they seek to exploit it in winning over adherents. However, it is one thing to use the university as a means of reforming society, and quite another to try to reform the university itself. It is better to use a tool, even if defective, to repair a machine than try to repair the tool and probably destroy the most effective and perhaps only means available to repair the machine.

Crucial to fulfilling the goals of a university is the principle of academic freedom. The call for radicalization has included attempts to bar from the campus those identified with the Establishment; this applies especially to those associated with the military, defense, and the War, i.e., R.O.T.C., Dow Chemical Company, military recruiting, and even spokesmen for orthodoxy. There are legitimate "educational" reasons in favor of extending or restricting certain activities on the campus, but it is quite apparent that the above attempted prohibitions are political or moral and thus incompatible with academic freedom. Assaults on academic freedom are not novel, but recent moves, in contrast to the past, originate from within the ivory tower rather than without. No segment of the campus should be permitted to tamper with it. Higher education has been so often faced (and still is) with the difficult task of protecting it from the community, that it ill behooves any members of the university to succumb to a similar temptation. The principle of academic freedom does not depend on the wisdom of experts; the converse is closer to the truth. It needs protection from even its greatest defenders and beneficiaries, who in a moment of passion may destroy one of the essential conditions for knowledge and learning. If the academic community abuses this right, it opens up a Pandora's box for those outside who would like an excuse to intervene and assault academic freedom.

Some schools have already begun to restrict certain student activities and even ban certain groups such as S.D.S. from campus participation. It is not difficult to arouse public intolerance toward groups whose rhetoric and actions reflect overt intolerance. Willingness to call the police to stem illegal and violent disruptions has spread from the public to university faculty and administrators.

Granted that the university should be guided by the principles of academic freedom and competence, it is ultimately responsible to the citizens in a democratic society. "Since educational institutions are generally regarded as serving a public function, and financed to a large extent by the general citizenry they ought to be responsible to the public."[34]

As citizens, members of the academic community have the right to employ whatever legal means are permitted to seek changes in education. Thus students, even if mistaken in judgment, have a right to request curricula reforms and more voice in the university. Competence does not guarantee infallibility and benevolence, and thus does not deserve exemption from suggestion and criticism.

"Decisions concerning academic standards and procedures

are generally made without so much as consulting students. This is not, I think, a healthy situation, and without indulging in any mystique about the spontaneous wisdom or virtue of the young, we ought to recognize the appropriateness of student consultation in academic affairs."[35]

The example of hospital patients is helpful here. Though patients are not expected to run a hospital or make the important decisions, they can offer constructive suggestions in certain matters within their capability. They ought to be consulted by the doctors and administrators. Similarly, students ought to be consulted in certain areas in which they have acquired information or formulated useful ideas and suggestions. In one sense, authorities ought to welcome suggestions from those outside their profession; this applies to faculty consulting not only students but those in the community at large, though there are, of course, practical limitations. But in another sense authorities have special reasons for consulting those connected with their fields, whether as patients, students, clients, customers, or consumers; their fields of specialization involve these individuals as important sources of information and an essential part of their subject matter. But there is confusion arising from the ambiguous function of "consulting." In one case, it refers to those who are consulted because they are experts in a particular field. In another case, it refers to those who are consulted by experts because they may be of help to experts. But this does not make the latter group being consulted experts in that particular field, though the former group being consulted are.

Though calls for student power sometimes stem from misunderstanding of democracy or revolutionary tactics, agitation is frequently founded on legitimate grievances, such as: poor teaching; overcrowded classrooms, eating facilities, and dorms; and excessive control over student activities (*in loco parentis*). The university is obliged to provide means for the expression of genuine complaints, and to investigate and respond to them, otherwise it makes for poorer education and unnecessary confrontations.

But it is also duty bound to uphold norms of competence, learning, and academic freedom, and not sacrifice them in response to intimidation, threats, illegal acts, or violence. Not every complaint is justified, not every request deserves to be met, and even where legitimate cannot be acceded to in an atmosphere of harassment or lawlessness. Even if appeasement could purchase temporary tranquillity on the campus, it might be over the corpse of higher learning.

FOOTNOTES

1. Henry B. Mayo, "An Introduction to Democratic Theory," Oxford University Press, 1960, reprinted in *Communism, Fascism & Democracy,* edited by Carl Cohen, Random House, 1962, p. 660.
2. Friedrich A. Hayek, "The Road to Serfdom," University of Chicago Press, 1944, reprinted in *ibid.,* p. 610.
3. M. Stanton Evans, *The Future of Conservatism,* Holt, Rinehart, and Winston, 1968, p. 293.
4. Henry Steele Commager, *Freedom and Order,* George Braziller, 1966, p. 120.
5. David Spitz, "A Liberal Perspective on Liberalism and Conservatism," *Left, Right and Center,* edited by Robert A. Goldwin, Rand McNally & Company, 1968, p. 24.
6. *Ibid.,* p. 23.
7. Leslie Lipson, *The Democratic Civilization,* Oxford University Press, 1964, p. 548.
8. John Dewey, *Freedom and Culture,* Capricorn Books, 1963, p. 71.
9. Leslie Lipson, *op. cit.,* p. 546.
10. John W. Gardner, *No Easy Victories,* Harper & Row, 1968, p. 149.
11. John Locke, *The Second Treatise of Government, 1690,* Liberal Arts Press, 1952, p. 54.
12. Leslie Lipson, *op. cit.,* p. 538.
13. John Dewey, *op. cit.,* p. 63.
14. S. I. Benn and R. S. Peters, *Social Principles and the Democratic State,* George Allen & Unwin, Ltd., 1959, p. 120.
15. William Ernest Hocking, *Strength of Men and Nations,* Harper & Brothers, 1959, p. 56.
16. S. I. Benn and R. S. Peters, *op. cit.,* p. 119.
17. John K. Galbraith, *The New Industrial State,* Houghton Mifflin Company, 1967, p. 241.
18. Arnold Schuchter, *White Power/Black Freedom,* Beacon Press, 1968, p. 10.
19. John W. Gardner, *op. cit.,* p. 61.

20. Henry B. Mayo, *op. cit.*, p. 656.
21. Jacques Barzun, *Teacher in America*, Little, Brown, and Company, 1944, p. 255.
22. William Ernest Hocking, *op. cit.*, p. 22.
23. Howard Mumford Jones, "The Meaning of a University," in *The Troubled Campus*, prepared by the editors of the *Atlantic*, Little, Brown, and Company, 1965, p. 180.
24. Jacques Barzun, *The House of Intellect*, Harper & Row, 1959, p. 130.
25. Clark Kerr, "The Frantic Race to Remain Contemporary," in *Revolution at Berkeley*, edited by Michael V. Miller and Susan Gilmore, Dial Press, 1965, p. 23.
26. Jacques Barzun, *Teacher in America*, op. cit., p. 34.
27. Irving Howe, "Berkeley and Beyond," in *Revolution at Berkeley*, p. xx.
28. William Clyde DeVane, *Higher Education in Twentieth-Century America*, Harvard University Press, 1965, p. 10.
29. John W. Gardner, *op., cit.*, p. 86.
30. Seymour M. Lipset, "Students and Politics in Comparative Perspective," *Daedalus*, Winter 1968, Vol. 97, No. 1, p. 14.
31. Richard E. Peterson, "The Student Left in American Higher Education," *Daedalus, op. cit.*, p. 313.
32. John W. Gardner, *op. cit.*, p. 89.
33. Seymour M. Lipset, *op. cit.*, p. 3.
34. James Ridgeway, *The Closed Corporation*, Random House, 1968, p. 215.
35. Irving Howe, *op. cit.*, p. xviii.

CHAPTER III

DEMOCRACY, LOYALTY, AND DISOBEDIENCE

I. Loyalty, Dissent, and Subversion

A society is expected to defend itself against those who wish to destroy it. Opposition to its right to protect itself reflects unconcern about its survival. Can we consistently support a democratic society and at the same time oppose measures to preserve its existence?

There are those who claim that implicit in a free society is freedom of belief and the right to dissent from prevailing opinions.

> If all mankind minus one, were of one opinion, and only one person were of the contrary opinion, mankind would be no more justified in silencing that one person, than he, if he had the power, would be justified in silencing mankind. Were an opinion a personal possession of no value except to the owner; if to be obstructed in the enjoyment of it were simply a private injury, it would make some difference whether the injury was inflicted only on a few persons or on many. But the peculiar evil of silencing the expression of an opinion is, that it is robbing the human race; posterity as well as the existing generation; those who dissent from the opinion; still more than those who hold it. If the opinion is right, they are deprived of the opportunity of exchanging error for truth: if wrong, they lose, what is almost as great a benefit, the clearer perception and livelier impression of truth, produced by its collision with error.[1]

The right to dissent extends even to those who are opposed to democracy. Any attempt to curb this right in order to protect democracy from its enemies, threatens democracy. Therefore, it is unfair to suggest that those who question its right to defend itself in this manner are apathetic about its survival.

We are then faced with a dilemma. If we fail to take steps to preserve democracy we endanger its existence. "As a contituted regime, democracy has the right to preserve itself. Liberty can be protected against abuses committed in its name. The German Nazis, Italian Fascists and Czechoslovak Communists demonstrated in this century the possibility of undermining from within the authority which safeguards freedom."[2] However, if we take measures to defend it we contribute to abolishing it. One way out of this dilemma is to consider which alternative poses the greater risk. But we have to make the alternatives more precise. All kinds of measures can be taken to protect a free society. There are also different concepts of democracy involved here.

The examples of Germany, Italy, and Czechoslovakia reflect the dilemma. Each of these countries, in the name of democracy, permitted totalitarian parties to function, which enabled them to seize power. This suggests that restrictions should have been instituted to prevent this. On the other hand, it was by instituting restrictions that the totalitarian parties were able to do away with democracy. This suggests that restrictions should not have been permitted. Thus, paradoxically, earlier restrictions might have saved democracy whereas later restrictions brought about its demise. One obvious way of resolving this paradox is to distinguish between the two kinds of restrictions involved. If these nations had originally banned only totalitarian parties, they might have prevented their growth and ultimate seizure of power. Thus the restrictions should be confined solely to "undemocratic" parties and organizations. There would be no restrictions on "democratic" parties. The later restrictions were imposed by the totalitarian party in power, on all other parties, democratic or totalitarian. In one case, restrictions applied only to totalitarian parties, in the other, to all parties save one.

Clearly, one can distinguish between a restricted one-party system and a restricted multi-party system. There is no more paradox here than there is in distinguishing between the use of force to prevent crime and its use in committing it, in the use of a sharp instrument (scalpel) to save life and its use to kill, and so on. Likewise, one can understand and distinguish the use of restrictions to prevent totalitarianism and its use to bring it about.

Now one may desire a country without restrictions on any party, totalitarian or democratic; one may prefer this to the above examples of restricted societies, whether one-party or multi-party. One may wish to confine the term "democratic" to the last of the three types of systems described above. But this does not eliminate the difference between the first two in the kinds of restrictions involved and in their purposes. Though the paradox may have been resolved, however, the question remains: What kind of restrictions, if any, are necessary for a democracy to defend itself and survive? Should totalitarian parties be banned, not be permitted to run candidates or hold office?

> Nevertheless, there is a point at which an anti-democratic party becomes dangerously large, when it employs its democratic rights to obstruct and discredit the democratic process, and when it threatens to become powerful enough to overturn it. At this stage the rights of the minority in question have to be weighed against the rights of all those who would be its victims. There is now a conflict of claims, including the claims of democracy itself. Though suppression may not provide a permanent solution to this problem in practice, it could conceivably be justified as a precaution while other remedies were given a chance to operate. If a restriction on minority rights could be effective in preserving democracy, it would be a misguided quixotry to oppose it.[3]

Though the examples of Germany, Italy, and Czechoslovakia might seem to support the affirmative here, the examples of England, France, and Sweden permitting totalitarian parties but nevertheless maintaining enduring democratic systems appear to represent contrary instances. Though the latter examples may merely be lucky exceptions, the former examples may be unlucky instances in which the cause of totalitarianism had nothing to do with permitting totalitarian parties to operate. If banning totalitarian parties is intended to prevent them from winning wider support legally and subsequently taking over, then this can be achieved as effectively without a ban. Through social reform, education, and propaganda, the public can be alerted to the dangers of totalitarianism. On the other hand, if the danger derives from treason, subversion, espionage, insurrections, and illegal and violent acts, there are means to deal with this without banning any party or organization. Inhibitions about outlawing parties should not prevent the government from taking appropriate steps against any individual or group for acts threatening the security of the nation or in violation of law.

Attempts to outlaw undemocratic parties raise problems of determining what is undemocratic, who shall administer it, dangers of abuse, and subterfuge of those banned under disguised and false banners. The lessons of McCarthyism in this country, and the litigation involving the Smith and McCarran Acts, indicate the futility and viciousness, with little to show in support of the security and democratic values of the nation.

Defending a free society against its opponents does not necessarily imply curbing the right of its enemies from dissenting. Excluding subversives from certain jobs or requiring loyalty oaths does not deprive anyone of the right of free speech. It may discourage some from expressing themselves with complete candor from fear of not obtaining or losing a job. But this is true of any requirements for employment. A person without the necessary qualifications might wish to hide this.

It may be suggested that the right to dissent is being severely limited by being subject to intimidation. This is incompatible with democracy. Free speech requires an atmosphere without fear of not being employed because one may be labeled a subversive or refuse to sign a loyalty oath. But suppose such measures do contribute to preventing the enemies of democracy from obtaining influence or power? Isn't a limited democracy better than no democracy at all? Isn't limited free speech better than no free speech? Isn't half a loaf better than none?

"If we destroy the freedom of the alleged erstwhile dictator very early in the game, we have chosen a present and sure limitation on democracy rather than risk an eventual and possible one. Surely this is to lose by forfeit. Of course, if we wait too long our loss may be even greater. But certainly we must wait long enough to discover whether the utterance does in fact threaten totalitarianism."[4]

That such steps as excluding subversives or requiring loyalty oaths are effective will be challenged. Preventing a subversive from obtaining an ordinary position will not stop him from attacking or advocating the overthrow of the democratic system or committing sabotage or treason. Expressing opposition to democracy does not mean that it will be destroyed. Holding an ordinary job does not increase the risk of sabotage or treason. Requiring loyalty oaths will not prevent one critical of democracy from signing them and hiding his beliefs or intentions.

Holding a security position does increase the opportunity for sabotage or treason. Here one can make a case for excluding certain individuals. There is still a problem of determining the kind of employment and the kind of persons to be subject to exclusion. It would be difficult to maintain that no one should be barred even if there were a danger to a democratic society. Though security clearance machinery is always subject to abuse, the clear and present dangers involved justify its priority over possible mistreatment to citizens applying for security positions. Here, the criterion deserves to be quite stringent, and membership in organizations deemed totalitarian in commitment should be sufficient against security employment. One cannot apply the adage that it is better that ten guilty men go free than that one innocent man be punished. Rather the contrary: It is better that ten innocent men be excluded from a security position than that one guilty man be hired.

But requiring loyalty oaths seems dubious even in security positions. If there is reason to doubt a person's fitness to hold a security position, a loyalty oath is unnecessary. If there is no reason to suspect an individual's loyalty, the oath is unnecessary. If one is disloyal, but there is no evidence to support this, he is not likely to expose his intentions by refusing to sign a loyalty oath. In this case, the oath is useless.

We believe that subversives should be barred from employment essential to the security of the country. There is little argument about jobs involving military secrets or defense plants, public or private. Some claim that our educational system is vital to the security of the country. Schools mold the thinking of youth, particularly those destined to be future leaders of society. Our teachers are the major vehicle for transmitting democratic values. Allowing subversives to teach is subjecting young minds to forces opposed to democracy. Teachers wield enormous influence over students and the community as a result of their prestige and position in society.

It will be said that the danger is minor. Most teachers are loyal. Their influence surely outweighs the few who are not. Students are affected by teachers, parents, newspapers, radio, churches, and other institutions committed to the democratic way of life. Even if a few students are subverted by those opposed to democracy, this is likely to be short-lived, particularly after they have left school. The country with a population overwhelmingly committed to democracy is in no danger from a handful who may have been subverted.

But the threat is not to be measured merely by numbers or by the likelihood of an immediate overthrow of our democratic society. We cannot ignore long-run considerations. Over a period of years or decades, even a few subversive teachers will be turning out a number of students each term committed to the overthrow of a free society. They will be trying to get into strategic places in industry, government, labor, churches, and education. In time of crisis or war, just a handful can do great damage. It is not being suggested that this would be fatal. But prudence dictates that we do the utmost to minimizes the danger by barring them from our schools.

Under present conditions of political and military warfare, it is not hard to see what immense dangers to the security of liberal institutions is implicit in this strategy of infiltration and deceit. Even a few men in sensitive posts can do incalculable harm. These instructions—and there are many more detailed ones combined with explicit directives to Communists to transform any war in which their country is involved, except one approved by the Soviet Union into a civil war against their own government—indicate that members of the Communist party are not so much heretics as conspirators and in actual practice regard themselves as such.[5]

One can hardly deny that recent campus disorders have been led by student revolutionaries stimulated by teachers dedicated to overthrow of the government by illegal and violent means, if necessary. There are teachers, particularly in higher education, who openly espouse and attempt to convert students to revolutionary opposition to American institutions and democracy itself. This is not confined merely to advocacy of revolution in the abstract or at some distant future. Major universities have been attacked, physically and violently, with the openly declared intention of paralyzing, shutting down, and destroying one of the fundamental institutions of our society. Teachers overtly declare their support of "resistance" to the government, the military, the draft; they openly recruit students and others to defy the government and to prepare for revolution. They repudiate our democratic institutions, the ballot box, majority rule, the constitution, the legislative bodies, and so on. Whether the issue be that of capitalism, racism, imperialism, or fascism, faculty members joined by students and others openly declare their intention to overthrow the Establishment. This has even penetrated the secondary schools, where attempts are made to win and recruit opposition to our whole system of government. New generations of graduate students are being absorbed into our educational system, committed to the destruction of our society. What can this all lead to in the long run?

How do we go about prohibiting subversives from teaching? How do we determine who they are, and who shall decide? Since we have been concerned with those opposed to democracy, it is reasonable for this purpose to classify anyone opposed to democracy as subversive. We are already faced with a problem, since not everyone will agree with this definition. How do we ascertain who is opposed to democracy, assuming that we can agree on what we mean by this? Is it merely a matter of someone stating that he is opposed to democracy? How many, if any, of those who really do not believe in democracy are likely to express this, particularly if they can expect to be excluded as subversive? Or is it a matter of discovering whether an individual belongs to an organization opposed to democracy? Can we expect such organizations to formulate their programs and policies so that they can be used as guides for exclusion?

Even organizations who openly proclaim "revolution" are rarely clear about what they mean. Differences among spokesmen and internal conflicts among factions concerning ideology, strategy, programs, and interpretation raise doubts whether any group can be definitely labeled as favoring illegal or violent overthrow of government. It is also not entirely clear how much of their language is rhetoric and tactical, intended to arouse and express strong feeling and create pressures for changes. If one examines the statements of the S.D.S., the Black Panthers, and Cleaver on the one hand, and the Minute Men, Ku Klux Klan, and the John Birch Society on the other, their vagueness, shifting positions, and diverse interpretations allow their members to read all sorts of positions into their writings. It seems a formidable task to prove that a particular organization to which a teacher belongs is in fact opposed to democracy. We can expect individuals and organizations to go underground, mask subversive intentions, and thus make it easier for subversives to teach with their real views and intentions hidden.

Who shall judge who is subversive? Can we entrust this to a political agency of the government, whether federal, state, or local? Can we expect political agencies to be immune to political pressures and personal ambitions in making such judgments? Even with best intentions, are they capable of making such decisions? Will they distinguish between heresy and subversion?

It may be suggested that teachers should be judged by their peers or those trained in education. They seem by virtue of their training and experience the most likely candidates for determining who is a subversive teacher. They are more familiar with the thinking and actions of their colleagues, more immune to political pressures, and more concerned with academic freedom. Who else is more capable of distinguishing between heresy and subversion? But are teachers invulnerable to personal rivalries and ambitions? Are they free of political pressures from both inside and outside the school systems? Will they be able to transcend their own personal biases and ideological commitments? It is one thing to ask them to evaluate other teachers' scholarly competence or teaching abilities. It is quite another to judge a person's political beliefs.

What consequences would investigations by either political agencies or educational institutions have for academic freedom? "What is the effect on the faculty and on the student body? Will professors be as free in the future as they have been in the past to explore dangerous ideas, to embark upon original research, to associate with nonconformists? Will students be as free as in the past to discuss whatever interests them, to join whatever organizations appeal to them, to test their intellectual muscles on controversial issues?"[6]

There are some teachers who would teach and write and speak in the same way, regardless of investigations. But there are others who, because of fear of being suspected or accused of subversion, would hesitate to express themselves freely and honestly. It would erode the atmosphere of learning and teaching and the quest for knowledge and trust. Students would realize that society lacks confidence and trust in their ability and judgment. It would encourage in students attitudes of inferiority, fear of free inquiry, and suspicion of teachers. It might encourage teachers and students to engage in accusations, spying, and even blackmail.

Some will say that we have to pay some price for eliminating subversives from the schools. It is worth suffering a loss of some academic freedom for the ultimate purpose of preventing a loss of all freedom, including academic freedom. Any law that restricts individuals runs the risk of abuse. We are obligated to see to it that machinery for eliminating subversives is not mishandled. We can provide mechanisms for appeal and for minimizing dangers to the innocent. But our primary duty is protecting democracy from its enemies.

One basic disagreement concerns the assessment of risk in permitting subversives to teach. We have suggested that the number of individuals who might be subverted is so small compared to the rest of the population that there is little to fear, even in the long run. Thus, even if the harm to academic freedom were practically nil, the case for excluding subversives has not been made. There are other ways to reduce the danger from opponents of a free society. Academic freedom can be exercised by defenders as well as critics of democracy. Institutions outside the schools, such as the government, press, radio, television, churches, and public forums are resources with virtually unlimited potential for espousing democratic values. Where necessary, further security measures can be taken by government agencies to protect society against treason or sabotage. Academic freedom does not exempt teachers from obeying laws, does not protect them from punishment or dismissal for treason or sabotage or breaking school regulations. Even their verbal behavior is subject to the limits of clear and present danger regulations. Where faculty are found to participate and encourage others in campus disruptions, to break the laws, to threaten or intimidate others, to destroy property, they can be subject to prosecution, dismissal, and punishment. The very attacks made on a free society can be turned to good use, by correcting those weaknesses which critics exploit against democracy. Energy needed to exclude subversives from schools might be better employed in defense of democracy without suffering the harmful effects to academic freedom.

We have been considering how a democracy might defend itself against its enemies in the area of employment. What about the area of public opinion? Does a democratic society have the right to expose individuals and organizations whose beliefs and programs are incompatible with democratic values? Does the government have the right to investigate and attack them for the purpose of alerting and influencing public opinion? Some hold that any government action to curb or attack subversive belief is incompatible with democracy. It is a form of intimidation which stifles freedom of dissent. The House Committee on Un-American Activities is characterized as follows: "For thirty years the most cherished ideals of liberalism and many of its heroes have been among the Committee's main targets. Liberals have had their motives impugned and their patriotism questioned. They have seen associates and acquaintances harried by investigators and have read of the ordeals of witnesses with whom they could easily identify."[7] A democratic society is committed to the free expression of ideas from all quarters, a tolerance for beliefs, however distasteful.

It is ironic to find Herbert Marcuse, a self-proclaimed

radical, questioning the belief in tolerance, and recommending that it be restricted to those who are "rational," capable of making judgments. He says: "This pure toleration of sense and nonsense is justified by the democratic argument that nobody, neither group nor individual, is in possession of the truth and capable of defining what is right and wrong, good and bad. Therefore, all contesting opinions must be submitted to 'the people' for its deliberation and choice. But I have already suggested that the democratic argument implies a necessary condition, namely that the people must be capable of deliberating and choosing on the basis of knowledge, that they must have access to authentic information, and that, on this basis, their evaluation must be the result of autonomous thought."[8]

The danger is perhaps greatest for thinkers like Marcuse, if any group were permitted to decide who is "rational" and therefore eligible to freely express his ideas; Marcuse would probably be one of the earliest victims. The toleration of differences is not based on the assumption that no one is capable of determining the truth or the good; rather, that entrusting anyone (including those capable of determining what is true or good) with power to restrict what can be expressed leads to the danger that the truth and the good will be suppressed. It is better to tolerate sense and nonsense than to risk the suppression of sense, either in the name of suppressing nonsense or by those who espouse nonsense. If the democratic argument presupposes as a necessary condition that the people must make "rational" choices on the basis of adequate knowledge, then unrestricted tolerance more closely approximates this condition than restricted tolerance. The search for knowledge is aided by permitting ideas from all sources, even if some turn out to be nonsense.

Is freedom of belief a privilege only for subversives? Shall we permit those opposed to democracy the right to criticize and expose the government and its policies, but deprive the government from the right to do the same? If subversives feel intimidated when attacked and exposed by the government, is this not also true for the government when attacked and exposed by subversives? The right to express ideas freely does not guarantee that one will not be judged unfavorably or even condemned. This is true for dissenters and subversives as well as the government and upholders of the *status quo*.

But we must distinguish between the mere expression of belief and action taken by the government against subversives. The government may have a right to expose and attack subversives by criticizing and condemning them. To deny it this right would constitute a limit on its free expression of ideas. But when the government holds hearings and subpoenas individuals, it goes beyond the realm of free speech. Criticism of government investigating bodies has been raised on two counts. Some have questioned the procedures used in investigating subversives and subversion. Valid objections can be raised against unfair methods of conducting hearings and investigations. This may involve the right of cross-examination, the right to confront one's accusers and the right to defend oneself against false accusations, libel, or slander. If the purpose of holding hearings is that of promoting belief in democratic values and minimizing the influence of subversives, then procedural abuses will hinder rather than help this goal.

Others have objected to the very principle of government investigations of subversives and subversion. It is a form of intimidation which goes beyond the mere expression of belief, and thus cannot be justified even if carried out in a completely fair manner. It is granted that investigations may be necessary for excluding subversives from security positions. But if they are held for the purpose of exposing subversives to the community or to influence public opinion, they appear unwarranted.

But doesn't a free society have the right to conduct hearings in order to discourage undemocratic beliefs? Can this goal be achieved as effectively without formal hearings? Is the fact that subversives may be subpoenaed helpful in obtaining information?

"Again and again Congressional committees have alleged that without information wrung from reluctant witnesses it would be impossible for Congress to legislate on matters of subversion. In many instances witnesses have preferred to go to jail rather than to give the information; has Congress in fact been unable to legislate in this area?"[9] Furthermore, are the investigations normally intended for gathering information for legislative purposes? "Public committee hearings, including investigations, are basically designed for dramatic and cathartic purposes, not to obtain needed information for Congress. That is precisely why the parades of witnesses, the exact content of whose testimony everybody knows in advance, are such a common feature of such hearings."[10]

Do such procedures promote greater publicity and are they more effective in influencing public opinion and fostering democratic belief?

It is difficult to deny that formal hearings are more dramatic than alternative means of attacking and exposing subversives. But it can be argued that subpoenaing witnesses lends itself to such abuse that it would be more just and effective to have hearings without forcing witnesses to testify.

It is claimed that the House Committee on Un-American Activities "has established a record not of laws but of Fifth Amendment pleas and contempt citations and disrupted lives. The proudest exhibit of the Committee's thirty years is its spacious files filled with the names, associations, activities, and public utterances of thousands of Americans."[11] Better means of influencing public opinion exist than coercing witnesses to appear before governmental bodies. This would have the advantage of not making martyrs out of them.

We have not considered the constitutional issues surrounding investigations of subversion. We have been primarily concerned with the wisdom and effectiveness of such investigations in promoting democracy. We believe that this should determine whether constitutional requirements are to be modified or retained.

II. *Is Civil Disobedience Warranted?*

Can those who believe in democracy support civil disobedience in a democratic society? An advocate of democracy could employ, without inconsistency, and with justification, illegal means to resist and even overthrow a despotic government. But may a democrat justifiably violate the laws in a democracy?

We are not alluding to "breaking a law" in order to test its constitutionality, since what is the "law" is itself at issue. One is obliged to challenge in court a law one sincerely believes unconstitutional, even at risk of violating the law if its constitutionality is upheld. This is essentially different from what we normally mean by "civil disobedience" where the law being broken is presumed constitutional.

"Civil disobedience is not a matter of challenging the legality of a law or of ascertaining the meaning of a law. It is a matter of a man rejecting a moral demand of his society at the same time that he admits the legal right of his society over him."[12] This is not to deny the ambiguity of its use, or to legislate how it shall be used. Frequently a civilly disobedient act intended as a moral challenge is transformed into a legal one involving constitutionality. This has occurred recently in opposition and resistance to the draft. It is not always clear whether a constitutional challenge is intended primarily to serve the same purpose as an act of civil disobedience, namely, publicity, moral outrage, jail sentence, etc., or whether the parties involved sincerely believe that a constitutional issue is at stake. Many activities down South by civil rights leaders in the 1960s were popularly described as acts of civil disobedience, though in conflict with local and state laws subsequently declared unconstitutional. Given the historical precedent concerning the law of the land, a believer in democracy ought perhaps to restrict the problem of civil disobedience to those acts not intended to challenge the constitutionality of laws or policies but their morality.

It seems that if we approve of the procedure by which laws are promulgated, we are obligated to obey them But a majority might sanction laws so unjust we would feel compelled to defy them.

"Unjust laws exist; shall we be content to obey them, or shall we endeavor to amend them, and obey them until we have succeeded, or shall we transgress them at once? Men generally, under such a government as this, think that they ought to wait until they have persuaded the majority to alter them. They think that, if they should resist, the remedy would be worse than the evil. But it is the fault of the government itself that the remedy *is* worse than the evil. *It* makes it worse. Why is it not more apt to anticipate and provide for reform? Why does it not cherish its wise minority?"[13] Is it the fault of government that the remedy is worse than the evil? At most, the government might be responsible for not preventing the remedy from occurring by promoting reform, but is not to blame for the remedy being worse than the evil. Perhaps this is what Thoreau meant. But this does not excuse the transgressors for supporting a remedy worse than the evil. Furthermore, if the transgression reflects their failure to persuade the majority to alter unjust laws, then the government is faced with a dilemma. Thoreau expects the government to respond to the minority even though the majority believes otherwise. If so, would the government then be responsible if the majority decided to resist, thinking that disobedience is apparently more effective in getting the government to act than legal processes? Who shall the government respond to, the majority or minority? How do we cope with this dilemma?

"If the morality of a democratic regime has to be derived from the consent of the governed, this cannot be reconciled with the rule of the majority. The dissenting minority exists. It cannot be explained away. If consent justifies a government's power, the inference follows that for those who withhold consent such powers are unjustified."[14]

If consent of the governed requires unanimity of the governed and thus cannot operate on majority rule because of minority dissent, then apparently democratic government operating on the principle of consent of the governed cannot operate at all. Some advocates of civil disobedience may accept Locke's interpretation of consent of the governed as reflecting majority rule and thus concede punishment of transgression as justified in a democratic society. Though acknowledging the principle of majority rule as just, they nevertheless recognize that this can sometimes lead to unjust laws that need to be resisted.

If justification for democracy is based on the belief that it is more beneficial to society than alternative political systems, it does not imply that every majority decision is preferable. It merely means the total advantage to society will be greater if governed democratically than by other means. But this is compatible with a particular majority decision being harmful to society.

"After all, the practical reason why, when the power is once in the hands of the people, a majority are permitted, and for a long period continue, to rule, is not because they are most likely to be in the right, nor because this seems fairest to the minority, but because they are physically the strongest. But a government in which the majority rule in all cases cannot be based on justice, even as far as men understand it."[15]

There is no contradiction in maintaining that, though the political process is sound, a particular law derived from the process is undesirable. But we cannot infer from this that we ought to break that law. Indeed, we normally expect supporters of democracy to abide by laws with which they disagree. Disobeying decisions of a majority reflects disdain for the very process of decision making, i.e., majority rule. Civil disobedience is interpreted as a sign of opposition to the political system itself, and thus inconsistent with belief in democracy.

We are expected to abide by the decisions of the process and to employ the process to attempt to change the decisions we oppose. We cannot guarantee that our own view will prevail, that it will be acceptable to the majority. This is part of what it means to practice democracy. What does it mean to believe in democracy if we are not prepared to accept the consequences of its political processes? We can perhaps avoid inconsistency if we do not believe "completely" in democracy. There are different kinds of commitment extending over a wide range from wholehearted and unqualified belief which may be incompatible with civil disobedience, to halfhearted, wavering, temporary, qualified, shifting belief, compatible with occasional transgressions.

In revulsion toward American policies on civil rights or Viet Nam, some have become disenchanted and have given up on democracy or majority rule; they cannot be accused of inconsistency in advocating civil disobedience. Others who profess to favor democracy no longer describe American society as democratic, and avoid inconsistency at the risk of ambiguity in the use of the term "democratic." If the absence of any law or policy deserving of civil disobedience becomes a defining characteristic of a "democratic" society, then one has made it true by definition that one resorts to civil disobedience only when a society is no longer "democratic"; therefore one cannot be accused of supporting civil disobedience in a "democratic" society. Indeed, they may claim that they are attempting by civil disobedience to restore "democracy" or bring it into fruition in our society. They may have a conception of democracy which is characterized primarily not by majority rule and constitutional rights, but by the fulfillment of certain ideals, such as peace, elimination of prejudice, abolition of poverty, and so on. They may have defined democracy as an ideal such that no state of affairs in the near future is likely to satisfy their definition. For them, there is no problem of reconciling civil disobedience with "democracy."

We must distinguish between two different situations. One may be opposed to a political system and indeed support its overthrow by illegal means, which does imply breaking its laws. It would be more accurate to refer to this as rebellion or revolution rather than civil disobedience, though some fall or vacillate between the two positions. On the other hand, one may be sympathetic to a political system, but find particular laws sufficiently repugnant to warrant disobeying them. It cannot be assumed that, because breaking laws sometimes reflects opposition to a political system, it always does.

"Some groups announce what are in effect total claims. Their members are obligated, whenever commanded, to challenge the whole established legal system, to overthrow and replace one government with another, to attack the very existence of the larger society. These are revolutionary groups. There are others, however, which make only partial claims. They demand that the larger society recognize their primacy in some particular area of social or political life and so limit its own. They require of their members disobedience at certain moments, not at every moment, the refusal of particular legal commands, not of every legal command."[16]

It may be argued that commitment to a political system implies that whatever interferes with, hinders, or contributes to the breakdown of that system is unwarranted, and, since civil disobedience does have that effect, it is inconsistent with support of the system. Proponents of civil disobedience who favor the political system are likely to deny that civil disobedience does have that effect, and thus reject the accusation of inconsistency. In contrast to more militant advocates, leaders like Martin Luther King have insisted that their commitment to nonviolent civil disobedience and acceptance of punishment represent, at most, nuisance value to arouse the conscience of society, hardly a threat to the foundations of government.

"The nonviolent resisters can summarize their message in the following simple terms: We will take direct action against injustice without waiting for other agencies to act. We will not obey unjust laws or submit to unjust practices. We will do this peacefully, openly, cheerfully because our aim is to persuade. We adopt the means of nonviolence because our end is a community at peace with itself. We will try to persuade with our words, but if our words fail, we will try to persuade with our acts. We will always be willing to talk and seek fair compromise, but we are ready to suffer when necessary and even risk our lives to become witness to the truth as we see it."[17] A distinction must be drawn between advocates of civil disobedience who believe it will cause the breakdown or overthrow of the political system, and those who sincerely doubt it.

The distinction between nonviolent and violent tactics which Martin Luther King tried so passionately to draw has had significant social and political consequences. Public fears of the threat to the system are especially aroused by destruction of property and even more so by violence and bloodshed. This is reflected in popular reaction to looting, rioting, and especially burning and sniping. The public finds it more difficult to disassociate the more militant, violent forms of disobedience from that of rebellion and revolution, a threat to the whole political system.

Though belief in civil disobedience is compatible with belief in majority rule, and belief in majority rule is compatible with disagreement with the majority, belief in civil disobedience is not implied by mere disagreement with the majority. We are faced with the crucial question: Under what conditions can one justify civil disobedience and yet support majority rule?

That a law is unjust does not constitute sufficient grounds for civil disobedience. Whenever we dissent from a law, we feel it is somewhat unjust. Whether civil disobedience is warranted depends on whether obeying the law will result in greater injustice than breaking it. If justification for civil disobedience is sought on the same basis as majority rule, namely, in terms of benefit or harm to society, then it will consist of ascertaining whether conforming to the law will be more harmful than violating it.

This is easier said than done. For it is one thing to argue that a particular law or policy is detrimental to society. It is quite another to show that breaking the law will result in less harm than obeying it. It is not at all obvious that breaking the law will diminish the enforcement or support of a law or policy, let alone do away with it. It may have the opposite effect, including prosecution and punishment of those engaged in civil disobedience.

Advocates of civil disobedience must judge whether their means are effective in achieving their ends. They assume they will be able to dramatize and publicize their moral indignation and their reasons for contempt. Even if their effort does not succeed immediately, in time they hope it will bear some fruit, however small, in its effect on public opinion and the law makers.

> The early Christians must have appeared singularly futile to their own generation when they challenged the majesty of Rome; but their steadfastness conquered the Western world. Luther's recalcitrance must have appeared akin to madness to a church which remembered its successful emergence from the stresses of the Conciliar revolt; but he changed the history of the world by his courage. Even so liberal a mind as Emerson could write of the American abolitionists that they were "narrow, self-pleasing, conceited men, and affected us as the insane do"; but it was hardly a generation afterwards that so respectable an observer as Oliver Wendell Holmes, not given to extreme views, could say of his friend's judgment that "it would have taken a long time to get rid of slavery if some of Emerson's teachings in that lecture had been accepted as the whole gospel of liberty."[18]

Civil disobedience is to be judged, then, by its success in the long run, if not in the immediate future. But since we cannot really be sure beforehand, and the final verdict will be rendered by hindsight, caution is called for in making any assessment about the appropriateness of civil disobedience. But even hindsight is a risky business, since it requires determining how subsequent events are related to preceding ones. That Christianity, Protestantism, and abolition of American slavery, all came to fruition, are in themselves no indication that prior acts of disobedience by Christians, Protestants, and abolitionists were important factors in their success. They may have succeeded *despite* the acts of disobedience. There were others besides the early Christians who resisted the Romans, yet did not finally triumph. The ideas of Christianity may have been more appealing than those of other groups. Many before Luther defied the Church but did not quite make his impact. Perhaps it was the period or personalities involved. There were many others besides the abolitionists who opposed slavery; ironically, disobedience (rebellion) by *supporters* of slavery (the South) contributed to the outbreak of the Civil War, and opponents of disobedience (the North) succeeded in abolishing slavery through that war. This may be a case where disobedience was counterproductive, where it boomeranged, resulting in the opposite effect of that intended.

All these movements were complex, involving many elements including disobedience; thus one cannot assume that the transgressions were the major causal factor. But even if this were the case, one must ask whether there were alternatives less costly than what is admittedly involved in acts of disobedience. That disobedience may have been sufficient in achieving the desired goal does not mean it was necessary, for other methods might have also been sufficient. Perhaps the Christians had little chance in the face of religious intolerance of the Roman Empire. Whether Luther might have avoided defying the Church by making accommodations in exchange for worthwhile concessions is rather difficult to settle. One doubts that the abolitionists foresaw or intended that their transgressions would provoke the South into its transgressions, thereby causing the Civil War, the Southern defeat, and the Northern imposition of the Emancipation Proclamation. But even if the abolitionists did contribute to marshaling and stirring support against slavery, which may have indirectly contributed to the firm stand of the North in the final confrontation, it is not clear how much of this was a consequence of disobedience by the abolitionists which might not have been also achieved by other means as well. Even if civil disobedience avoids being counterproductive and even if it succeeds one can ask whether the goal might not have been approximated by means less costly. This is especially so the more democratic the society, the more options are available for publicity, propaganda, politics, and persuasion.

Supporters of civil disobedience may believe that society will be no worse off if they try and fail and it will be better off if they succeed even a bit. They may maintain that even if the means they employ are not effective or have the opposite effect, the evil they oppose is so great that it makes little or no difference if they break the law. They will at least have the personal satisfaction of having been on the side of "good" and having resisted "evil." It should be noted that if one believes that civil disobedience will have the opposite effect from that intended, such a position would be inconsistent with the view that one's action should be aimed at increasing the benefit or reducing the harm to society.

More important is the availability of alternatives which are at least equally productive in attaining the desired goal as breaking the law. "The situation, it is said, is different in a state of which the form is a constitutional democracy. There, at any rate, freedom to criticize exists; and provision is deliberately made for those who differ from the government of the day to take its place if they can persuade a majority of their fellow citizens to vote with them. There is, I think, a vital truth in this view. In general, it is impossible to condone the use of violence in politics except as a weapon of last resort; it must be shown that all alternative avenues of action have been exhausted before violence is resorted to."[19] If dramatizing and publicizing the issue can be achieved by "lawful" demonstrations, picketing, printed literature, etc., then its relative effectiveness must be given serious consideration. Even if arrests produce wider public awareness than legal measures, it may not be more effective in achieving the end.

Those who believe civil disobedience more productive than legal dissent are in an unenviable position. If the law or policy being protested has strong popular support, both legal and illegal objections are likely to be met with public disfavor. However, illegal forms of dissidence have an additional burden, namely, that of public outrage at lawlessness, the diversion of the public's attention from the "evil" of the law or policy to that of the "illegal" character of the protesters. On the other hand, legal forms of protest are more likely to focus the public's attention exclusively on the "evil." Even if the law or policy being opposed does not have strong popular support, the same considerations would seem to indicate that illegal means will be less effective than legal means.

It may be thought that publicity is worth public outrage. Perhaps the moral intensity, the commitment and dedication, the courage and self-sacrifice reflected in the willingness to risk punishment will impress segments of the population and arouse them to look more closely at the issues. That people are willing to go to jail will surely convince some that important moral issues are at stake and win some adherents, even if merely to provoke them into engaging in legal activities. But one need not deny this in suggesting that it may arouse far more antipathy than sympathy. Is the acquisition of, let us say, ten supporters, worth the acquisition of one hundred adversaries? Would it not be preferable through legal means to win only five adherents but antagonize only fifty people? Given a society in which dissent may be expressed in a variety of ways, is it not possible to dramatize and publicize, on a large scale, almost as effectively as through sensationalism associated with civil disobedience? This requires money, time, and patience, and some dedicated activists may lack some or all of these. It is cheaper for a dozen committed to block a troop train and have this incident reported in the afternoon newspapers and evening television news cast across the land, than to buy comparable space in all the media. It is, of course, faster. And surely this precious thing called patience in the face of adversity is not helped by the emotional satisfaction of defying the law and being thrown in prison. It feeds and renews the commitment in a way that legal forms of dissent apparently cannot match. On the other hand, what is good for the goose is good for the gander; the public may indeed get the message of the transgressors and turn into a wild beast out to crush the law breakers.

Some supporters of civil disobedience believe that illegal disruptions or obstructions yield concessions toward their ultimate goals. However, fear by authorities that acceding under duress encourages further threats, and from other groups as well, produces contrary results, including a crack down in the name of law and order. Conceding that antagonism may be aroused by civil disobedience, some defend it, arguing that "An increase in immediate public hostility should not bring panicky abandonment of a tremendously powerful educational tool."[20] No doubt, civil disobedience possesses unique educational potential for winning adherents, particularly in the long run. But there is the other side to be calculated. In the United States, evidence of backlash and antagonism toward protests over civil rights and Viet Nam casts serious doubt on the utility of civil disobedience, not only in failing to win support from those elements who might otherwise be sympathetic, but in arousing opposition from those tending to be indifferent and provoking greater resistance from those opposed to the protests from the very beginning. Thus, in terms of effectiveness, the case for preferring civil disobedience over legal alternatives is difficult.

Some may read increased American opposition to the Viet Nam War as evidence for the effectiveness of disobedience. They assume that antagonism might not have developed as greatly without disorders. They suggest that mere legal forms of dissent to the War might not have increased the resistance. They seem to ignore the effect of time in war on people, particularly when "victory" appears to be continually out of reach, and casualties keep rising endlessly. They may grant that legal protest and war weariness play some role in increasing opposition, but they would have been far less effective without the stimulation and encouragement of civil disobedience. But how many war opponents are notwithstanding hostile toward the law breakers? How many skeptics about the war are nevertheless turned off by linking acts of disobedience with disrespect for all authority, all order, all legal process? How many individuals find themselves swayed emotionally to defend the government and the war when faced with emotional, hysterical, and abusive acts connected with trespassing, destruction of property, chaining bodies to buildings, burning draft cards, and so on?

A few are prepared to label any war critics as un-American, subversive, or traitors. But it would be difficult to persuade many that citizens and senators exercising their constitutional right to dissent were really enemies of the state. How different this is for law breakers who can easily be smeared as revolutionaries, anarchists, and worse.

Developments in civil rights could hardly have sustained the view of civil disobedience proponents, since increased civil disorders seemed to coincide roughly with greater opposition to civil rights A few were prepared to make concessions to defiers of the law. But there was little doubt that the majority were shifting the direction in which the country had been moving for many decades even prior to the 1954 Supreme Court desegregation decision. Even if new support for blacks could be attributed to disobedience, the antipathy aroused exceeded it overwhelmingly. Liberal activists and civil rights participants dropped out of the movement, became alienated and even hostile. Many who were indifferent became politically aroused against civil rights, began to join anti-civil rights groups, joined in demonstrations and political campaigns, including the Wallace for President movement which won approximately ten percent of the national vote cast in 1968. That some blacks became more militant, more violent, that rioting, looting, and burning had taken place, may have given some advocates of disobedience a false sense of "success," for these acts made conditions even worse by strengthening the forces against civil rights even more. One by-product of the shift in political winds which is perhaps more significant is that these "conservative" forces were able and willing to resist, reduce, and remove other programs dear to the disobedience proponents, including health, education, and welfare reforms.

Some advocates of civil disobedience are not impressed by questions of relative effectiveness, particularly where they believe it will have no significant effect, if any, in impeding or removing the law or policy. They argue that they are willing to or have tried to exhaust legal means, but have good reason to believe it cannot succeed or make much difference. In America, a few, disappointed in the accomplishments in civil rights and the escalation of the war in Southeast Asia, concluded that the time had come to move from legal to illegal forms of protest. Pragmatic considerations of effectiveness become irrelevant or pointless and they are faced with the burning question of "conscience" in the face of an intolerable evil. They maintain that the appeal to "conscience" has a time-honored tradition on fundamental moral questions. Every human being has a right to follow the dictates of his conscience in such matters. Surely, they ask, whether or not we agree with them, shouldn't we respect their right of freedom of conscience in refusing to obey?

"Can there not be a government in which majorities do not virtually decide right and wrong, but conscience?—in which majorities decide only those questions to which the rule of expediency is applicable? Must the citizen ever for a moment, or in the least degree, resign his conscience to the legislator? Why has every man a conscience, then? I think that we should be men first, and subjects afterward. It is not desirable to cultivate a respect for the law, so much as for the right. The only obligation which I have a right to assume, is to do at any time what I think right."[21]

However, this appeal to conscience can boomerang since

opponents of civil disobedience can likewise appeal to conscience, and law, as giving them the right to punish severely acts of civil disobedience. This is reflected in punitive governmental acts against rioting, draft-card burning, and interference with Selective Service processes. Furthermore, the policies and laws against which civil disobedience is being invoked can also be supported by appeals to conscience.

Interestingly enough, some civil disobedience proponents accept the "backlash" argument, conceding the right of their adversaries to respond likewise to their own consciences. A few are so convinced of their moral position they believe they will ultimately triumph in a "clash" of consciences. Others contend that their opponents, through legal means, have already put into practice what is in accord with their consciences; these include the very laws or policies which have provoked civil disobedience. But this means that the right to act in accordance with one's conscience does not imply that one's conscience is right. It also suggests that to act in accordance with one's belief is somehow moral even if the act is immoral and the belief is immoral.

"In saying that a person is a genuine conscientious objector, we say nothing about the objective correctness or incorrectness of his judgments but only that he has made them reflectively and honestly and is prepared to stand by them. What is 'conscience,' after all, but our blanket name for the personal governing principles to which a man is ultimately committed? We honor those who 'obey their conscience,' and we call it a moral (sometimes even religious) duty to do so. We revile those who knowingly do not do so."[22]

Apparently, we attach value to acting honestly and courageously as well as speaking so, to obeying our conscience as well as expressing it. We look with disfavor upon those who hide their beliefs as a reflection of untruthfulness and cowardice. Presumably, similar disdain applies to those who do not act in accordance with their principles. On the other hand, we recognize the value of controlling our impulses and desires; we admire and respect people who obey rules and laws they do not approve or like. Are we to condemn a man who obeys a law which violates his "principles," unless he happens to adopt the "principle" of obeying laws of which he disapproves, in which case we admire him for acting in accord with his "principles"? Perhaps it is courage and honesty to which we attribute value. Nevertheless, if proponents of civil disobedience can invoke conscience as grounds for performing an illegal act, there is no act, including murder, that could not be excused in similar fashion. Surely something has gone wrong here, since no one, including most advocates of civil disobedience, would wish to accept such a conclusion, and yet there is some sense in which we acknowledge the right to freedom of conscience.

Some confusion is derived from the meaning or use of the phrase "freedom of conscience." One sense in which we normally recognize this phrase as having positive value, is linked with such phrases as freedom of thought, opinion, belief, speech, etc. The right of freedom of conscience is understood to reflect the right to be free to hold or express any belief or opinion. Sometimes we even provide legal means for acting in accordance with one's convictions, e.g., a conscientious objector granted exemption from bearing arms. But this does not mean that one always has the right to act in accordance with one's belief. A person may have the right to believe in killing for mere pleasure, in overthrowing the government, or in racial discrimination, but this does not imply that he has the right to kill for mere pleasure, to overthrow the government, or to discriminate. This is merely to make the well-known distinction between belief and action, and our commitment to "freedom of conscience" refers to the former, not the latter.

However, under certain conditions, even expression of belief may constitute an illegal act, for "every speaker is free to say what he pleases unless and until his speech is so closely connected to illegal action that it becomes part of illegal action. Surely, no matter how absolute a defender of freedom of speech one may be, that defense cannot include protection for speech which is part and parcel of criminal action."[23]

In the context of civil disobedience, we acknowledge the

right of a person to "believe" in breaking a law, not the right to break a law. Thus to invoke freedom of conscience in refusing to obey a law is to confuse freedom of belief with freedom of action. It may be right to break a law, but not merely on the grounds of freedom of conscience.

It is, of course, not always clear where speech ends and action begins. It may be tempting, if only because it is less difficult, to classify an event as a symbolic part of speech if one favors it and part of action if one opposes it. This struggle has been reflected in recent incidents of draft-card and flag burning and draft resistance. Given these blurred situations, it is understandable that some will interpret "conscience" as applicable to actions as well as speech. Since these frequently involve litigation involving the Bill of Rights, appeals to conscience may be looked upon as a defense of basic constitutional rights. Occasionally what starts out as disobedience is transformed into a constitutional question. Thus, Dr. Benjamin Spock was accused of participating in a conspiracy to violate the draft laws by encouraging others to turn in their draft cards and refuse induction. The Spock case, involving appeals to conscience and reflecting resistance to the draft and opposition to the Viet Nam War, became a constitutional challenge of the Selective Service Law for violating Spock's right of free speech. What makes this case difficult is that, whereas one may grant the right to dispute the constitutionality of any law (and indeed this is not normally classified as civil disobedience), Spock originally indicated quite clearly that he intended to break the law, not challenge its constitutionality. However, it turned out to be a test case for drawing the line between speech and action.

Although we have characterized civil disobedience as consisting of breaking a law for some moral purpose or in order to resist some alleged injustice, the law being broken is not necessarily the law believed to be unjust. If one refuses to be drafted because he is against the draft, then the law being broken coincides with the law believed to be unjust. But if one opposed to the draft violates a trespassing law by sitting in at the Selective Service Board, the draft is the alleged "evil," not the law being broken. In either case, breaking a law is a means of promoting a moral end or resisting an alleged injustice. This means that if civil disobedience is to be justified, it must be shown that the end being promoted is moral or just, or that what is being resisted in unjust, not merely that the "conscience" of the advocate of civil disobedience impels him to believe this.

FOOTNOTES

1. John Stuart Mill, *On Liberty,* reprinted in *Communism, Fascism & Democracy,* edited by Carl Cohen, Random House, 1962, p. 554.
2. Leslie Lipson, *The Democratic Civilization,* Oxford University Press, 1964, p. 532.
3. S. I. Benn and R. S. Peters, *Social Principles of the Democratic State,* George Allen & Unwin Ltd., 1959, p. 354.
4. Martin Shapiro, *Freedom of Speech: The Supreme Court and Judicial Review,* Prentice Hall, 1966, p. 53.
5. Sidney Hook, "Heresy, Yes—Conspiracy No!" reprinted in *Contemporary Moral Issues,* second edition, edited by Harry K. Girvetz, Wadsworth, 1968, p. 90.
6. Henry Steele Commager, *Freedom and Order,* George Braziller, 1966, p. 84.
7. Walter Goodman, *The Committee,* Farrar, Straus and Giroux, 1968, p. 516.
8. Herbert Marcuse, "Repressive Tolerance," in *A Critique of Pure Tolerance,* by R. P. Wolff, B. Moore, Jr., H. Marcuse, Beacon Paperback, 1969, pp. 94–95.
9. Henry Steele Commager, *op. cit., p.* 39.
10. Martin Shapiro, *op cit.,* p. 168.
11. Walter Goodman, *op. cit.,* p. 519.
12. Darnell Rucker, "The Moral Grounds of Civil Disobedience," in *Ethics,* Vol. 76, January 1966, p. 143.
13. Henry David Thoreau, "On the Duty of Civil Disobedience," reprinted in *Social and Political Philosophy,* edited by John Somerville and Ronald E. Santoni, Anchor Books, Doubleday and Company, 1963, p. 289.
14. Leslie Lipson, *op. cit.,* p. 551.
15. Henry David Thoreau, *op. cit.,* p. 283.
16. Michael Walzer, "The Obligation to Disobey," in *Ethics,* Vol. 77, April 1967, p. 167.
17. Martin Luther King, Jr., "Where Do We Go From Here," in *Con-*

temporary Moral Issues, second edition, edited by H. Girvetz, Wadsworth Publishing Co., 1963, p. 46.
18. Harold Laski, "The Case for Disobedience," in Girvetz, *op. cit.,* p. 30.
19. *Ibid.,* p. 32.
20. Bradford Lyttle, "On Nonviolent Obstruction," in *Seeds of Liberation,* Edited by Paul Goodman, George Braziller, 1964, p. 128.
21. Henry David Thoreau, *op. cit.,* p. 283.
22. Carl Cohen, "Conscientious Objection," *Ethics,* Vol. 78, July 1968, p. 276.
23. Martin Shapiro, *op. cit.,* p. 123.

CHAPTER IV

CONSERVATISM, LIBERALISM, AND REVOLUTION

I. *Conservatism and Liberalism*

Are the positions of conservatism and liberalism clear, consistent, distinguishable, defensible, or even relevant to the contemporary political scene? Are they fruitful in resolving fundamental political, economic, and social problems, or do they constitute ideological and psychological impediments to critical thinking and creative solutions?

Though historically signifying a variety of things to different individuals, societies, and ages, conservatism has been generally associated with preserving and continuing the values of the past while liberalism has been identified with changing and reforming values in creating a different future.[1] In short, one is committed to the *status quo*, the other to change.

"Liberalism, it is said, seeks and promotes change; it is the party of something called progress. Conservatism fears and resists change; it is the party of stability. Where one stands in relation to the status quo is in this view the crux of the matter."[2]

It might seem that it is worth preserving a good society and changing a bad society, and, therefore, supporting conservatism in the former case and liberalism in the latter. On the other hand, even a good society can be improved and a bad society made worse, and therefore a case might be made for supporting the opposite positions. However, since the *status quo* is neither inherently good nor bad, one cannot determine what is worth preserving or changing without a critical evaluation of the *status quo*.

There are conservatives who believe that the *status quo* has superiority or priority in the absence of good reasons for change. That some procedure or rule or custom has been followed, that a tradition has been established is alleged to be a good and even sufficient reason for continuing it. There are liberals, on the other hand, who believe that unless the continuation of past procedures can be justified, change must be constantly encouraged in order to experiment, find better ways, new ideas, improve man's lot, and ameliorate the evils besetting humanity. They claim that change is itself a key to progress, to discovery, to acquiring new knowledge, and constitutes good and even sufficient grounds for support. The issue is joined here. Is any rule, in the absence of reasons for or against it, worth continuing or changing, for the sake of tradition or change? Is it possible to answer such a question in general or is it necessary to examine each case independently before one can properly assess it? Do we in practice ever find customs or laws which we can give no reasons for or against? People may find it difficult to make assessments, particularly in more complex cases, and may thus fall back on some general decision—making formula, i.e., tradition (or change), for its own sake. On the other hand, one may prefer to suspend judgment until or unless further evidence resolves the question. This is perhaps the most difficult position to adopt. Relying on the judgment of authorities involves choosing among them on the basis of their particular "liberal" or "conservative" stance; this reverts to the original problem of finding a basis for choosing.

In contemporary America, liberalism has been associated with attempts to revise the deficiencies of capitalism, by employing the government in a general reshuffling or redistribution of economic power and resources. Conservatism has been linked with preserving capitalism by resisting government intervention in the economic order.

Conservatives "believe that the modern state is politically so strong, even without controls over the economy, that it concentrates power to a degree that is incompatible with the freedom of its citizens. When to that power is added control over the economy, such massive power is created that the last defenses against the state becoming a monstrous Leviathan begin to crack."[3] This conforms to the liberal commitment to change and conservative commitment to the *status quo*. Thus liberalism has been identified with "big federal government," and conservatism with little (if any) government, though this is an oversimplification.

"In general discourse, however, 'conservatism' has become a passable designation for those who resist the extension of Federal authority. By the same token, I use the word 'liberal' to mean the point of view which favors centralization of power in Washington."[4] Naturally, conservatism has been identified with the "haves" or wealthy few with a stake in preserving capitalism, and liberalism with the "have-nots" or many poor with a stake in revising the economic order.

"Here liberalism, or the Left, is identified with that party associated with and representative of the interests of the lower classes, while conservatism, or the Right, is the party associated with and representative of the interests of the upper or dominant class."[5]

Though liberals have supported and conservatives have opposed the growth and intervention of government in economic affairs, paradoxically they have taken opposite positions with respect to civil liberties, dissent, subversion, and military defense. Their view of government was not always helpful in distinguishing them; even their attitude toward the *status quo* created confusion in light of the changes which in time became part of the *status quo*. Liberals found themselves in the position of defending those parts of the *status quo* they had helped achieve, while conservatives were supporting changes in the direction of the previous state of affairs.

A common thread which might serve as distinguishable criterion is the commitment to the privileged few (conservatives) in contrast to the less fortunate many (liberals). This would tend from a democratic viewpoint to load the case in favor of liberalism, except that the right commitment or good intentions are no substitute for intelligence and sound judgment; even the wrong commitment might have sound arguments of value to those with the right commitment. Thus, liberal emphasis on "bigger" government and unions, however justified in remedying deficiencies of private enterprise, was faced with abuse, waste, and corruption, which conservatives were only too happy to point out and exaggerate. Both liberals and conservatives tended to develop fixed or generalized attitudes toward the role of government which became substitutes for critical evaluation and "evidence" for particular programs.

In time, liberals found themselves shifting from support of the nonprivileged many to the even more nonprivileged few, and conservatives from support of the privileged few to the privileged many. This is reflected more recently in the battles over civil rights and particularly conditions among the underprivileged in the ghettos.

In earlier years, liberals supported broad segments who had suffered from the 1929 depression and who constituted a nonprivileged many. But liberal success in the rise and development of a strong labor union movement and New Deal legislation lifted broad sections of the underprivileged into a higher economic level, leaving large segments of blacks at the bottom of the scale. Most recently liberals have found themselves involved in the problems of the ghetto, and have lost support of elements of organized labor and professionals who have joined more conservative forces. Thus the liberals could no longer claim that they were supporting the many against the few, though they could maintain that they were continuing their support for the underprivileged in contrast to conservative support for the more privileged.

But the tables were turned, since the conservatives seemed to have captured the support of the majority from the liberals. Politically this is a weapon by which fundamental policies are shaped. Just as the privileged few in the past had learned or at least were forced to submit to the will of the majority, the underprivileged few most recently are faced with a majority not prepared to accede to all their demands, however just. The shift of a majority to conservatism fit in with the criterion of tradition versus change, the *status quo* having support of a privileged majority and reforms being urged by an underprivileged minority. The overlapping of these two criteria, tradition versus change, and privileged versus underprivileged, was a natural one, since the underprivileged needed changes to improve their conditions and the privileged had a stake in maintaining the *status quo*.

The distinction based on support for the upper and lower classes must not be pushed too far, since both conservatives and liberals have defended their positions as being of value to all the people, rich and poor. However, ideological dogma, passionate convictions, politics, and psychological associations with certain labels and slogans have interfered with objective and independent judgment of complex issues. Merely calling someone "conservative" or "liberal" evokes praise or condemnation, without considering the relative merits apart from labels or name-calling. Even if the conservative maintained that his position would be helpful to the underprivileged, what he said was looked on with suspicion by the liberal and underprivileged. Likewise, where the liberal suggested that his program would benefit the privileged, he was considered suspect by conservatives and privileged. The labels "liberal" and conservative" have continually kept getting in the way.

Conservatives and liberals accused each other of inconsistency, hypocrisy, dishonesty, or worse by their paradoxical positions toward the role of government in economic affairs and in civil liberties. Conservatives who had castigated government intervention in business as unconstitutional, undemocratic, and un-American were prepared to support government investigations of subversion in education, unions, and even business.

Ironically, "those who professed to fear government and who cherished individual rights voted—in 1940, in 1950, and in 1954—for ever stricter security measures, ever more comprehensive surveillance of associations, education, reading, travel, and even beliefs of citizens."[6] Liberals who had praised government intervention in industry and agriculture as truly democratic, constitutional, and for the public good condemned attempts by the government to set up machinery and procedures to ferret out subversion and treason as totalitarian and unconstitutional.

The apparently paradoxical attitude toward the role of government could perhaps be explained by the ends they sought. For conservatives, protecting the interests of the economically privileged entailed resisting government intervention in the economy while encouraging government interference with "radical" criticism of the economic system. However, it was more politically effective, even if lacking in candor, for conservatives to invoke the cry of individualism and constitutionalism in protecting the upper classes and invoking the cry of subversion and un-Americanism in attacking the "radicals." But this made conservatives vulnerable to the accusation of supporting the upper classes. Even where legitimate objections could be raised to excesses of government interference with privileged individuals, and a plausible case could be made for preventing subversion or treason, conservatives were suspect.

For liberals, aiding the underprivileged entailed supporting government intervention in the economy while resisting government interference with "radical" criticism of the economic system. But liberals described their support of government intervention as reflecting the voice of the people, democracy in action, and their opposition to government interference with "radicalism" as being in the tradition of constitutionalism and individual rights. This made them vulnerable to the accusation of supporting government bureaucracy and socialism, and apologists for subversion and even treason. Even where legitimate concern could be raised over excesses of capitalism and violations of civil liberties and dissent, liberals were suspect.

In foreign affairs, conservatives and liberals have also had opportunity to accuse each other of inconsistencies. Liberals who had been supporters of intervention, "hawks" during the rise of fascism have appeared to move toward a new isolationism, "doves" during the current conflict with communism. Conservatives who had been noninterventionist and isolationist during early days of fascism have been leading interventionists and "hawks" during the Cold War conflict.

"In their devotion to Western civilization and their unashamed and unself-conscious American patrotism, conservatives see Communism as an armed and messianic threat to the very existence of Western civilization and the United States. They believe that our entire foreign and military policy must be based upon recognition of this reality."[7]

Too many were supporting policies because it was the "liberal" or "conservative" thing to do, rather than because the policies could be sustained without regard to labels or ideologies. Enchantment with labels extended to slogans and policies associated with liberalism and conservatism, such as intervention and nonintervention, peacemonger and warmonger, appeasement and aggression, and so on. Conservatives who had been opposed to government growth and high taxes in connection with the domestic economy and foreign threat of fascism were quite willing to support military expansion and higher defense costs in resisting communism. Liberals who had supported larger governmental expenditures in domestic affairs and resistance to fascism, raised objection to growth of government and military expenditures in resisting communism.

It is ironic to hear conservatives invoke similar arguments against appeasement and aggression of communism that liberals used against fascism. It is also ironic to hear liberals repeat the criticism of foreign intervention against communism that conservatives used of intervention against fascism. These switches in roles left liberals vulnerable to attack as soft on communism and conservatives vulnerable to attack as soft on fascism, though both charges were clearly unfair, distorted and exaggerated. Undoubtedly some conservatives obsessed with the *status quo* considered fascists less menacing than communists, since the latter constituted apostles of change and the former proclaimed an anticommunist stance. Similarly, some liberals obsessed with commitment to change considered communists less dangerous than fascists, since the latter seemed to represent a bulwark against change and the former an ideology opposed to the *status quo*. Furthermore, association of fascism with the upper classes and communism with the lower classes seemed to be in accord with conservative commitment to the privileged and liberal commitment to the underprivileged.

In practice, of course, the fascists and communists were deadly to both privileged and nonprivileged; the fascists had little respect for conservative traditions; the communists had antipathy for liberal reforms. Most significant was their totalitarian nature which contradicted the democratic ethos of most conservatives and liberals. But the fact that the practices of fascism and communism were occurring outside the United States obscured their danger from many conservatives and liberals.

Here again, doctrinaire attitudes toward labels and slogans, such as the *status quo* and change, privileged and nonprivileged, blinded some conservatives and liberals into accepting general positions and policies without regard to particular facts and objective and independent inquiry.

In matters of academic freedom, liberals who were quite vituperous about the right of dissent and permitting communists to teach, have been prepared to ban Dow Chemical, the CIA, and military recruiters from campuses, whereas conservatives who have felt that academic freedom does not encompass the protection of "subversives" are in complete support of groups like Dow, the CIA, and military recruiters.

In civil rights, liberals who had insisted on the sanctity of constitutional rights of all citizens and condemned lawless and unconstitutional performances of segregationists, justified and engaged in civil disobedience pertaining to civil rights, the draft, and the Viet Nam War. Conservatives who had evaded and defied Supreme Court decisions on civil rights, school desegregation, open housing, equal job opportunities, bible reading, etc., in the name of states' rights, Americanism, and individualism, have been calling for law and order, the Constitution, security of the state, in the face of rioting, looting, and civil disobedience.

Granted there were exceptions in both camps, there were nevertheless sufficient adherents to the "party line" to constitute evidence that decisions were being made on a basis of labels and slogans reflecting doctrinaire attitudes. Even where the "party line" kept changing and both camps exchanged tactics and slogans, many adherents failed to realize this; these paradoxical shifts could be resolved by recognizing that the slogans or doctrines were means rather than ends, invoked by each side no matter that the other side had also employed them.

Recently, liberals have moved away from the doctrine of central planning toward decentralization, particularly in dealing with poverty, jobs, and education. Thus, "the question of halting the trend to centralization by getting power back into the hands of the states and local communities—is precisely the point on which the liberal intellectuals are moving most notably toward the conservative position."[8]

But since the primary motive of liberals was to help the underprivileged, particularly blacks in the ghettos, conservatives saw the call for decentralization as a threat to the privileged; they could be expected to shift the "line" accordingly, and come out, if not for centralization, at least against decentralization. It was ironic to find liberals supporting local and community control of schools and antipoverty programs and conservatives opposing it. Historically this is not a novel situation, for during the eighteenth and nineteenth centuries, conservatives were identified with strong central government while liberals were associated with states' rights and local control.

Both conservatives and liberals have reflected paradoxical postures toward the Constitution and the Supreme Court in fulfilling its function of judicial review.

"The Supreme Court, which southern politicians had, in fine conservative phraseology, defended so passionately from Roosevelt's clutches in 1937, now became a prime target. Those who had been opponents of the Court in 1937 also swapped weapons; liberal law professors began to talk, like Edmund Burke, about the beauties of tradition."[9]

It is understandable and not inconsistent to seek favorable court rulings. But each group has tried to have it both ways by defending and attacking the sacredness of the Constitution and judicial review on a basis of court decisions.

"During and after the New Deal, the liberals attacked the Court increasingly in the name of executive pre-eminence. But after this long history of hostility to judicial review, liberals, like conservatives, have greatly changed their position. It seems clear that principle regarding the Court has yielded in part, at least, to considerations of substantive policy. Liberals now like and conservatives now dislike what the Court is doing. Both seem to change regarding the Court according to their respective estimates of whether their policies will prevail."[10]

Thus, liberals attacked the Constitution and principle of judicial review when the Courts rendered conservatively oriented decisions, and conservatives responded in like manner to liberally oriented decisions. Whereas in the past, some liberals wished to "pack" the Supreme Court and abolish judicial review, recently some conservatives have attempted to limit the Supreme Court's powers and even impeach some of the judges.

"Conservatives who defended and liberals who attacked the Supreme Court in the 1930's have now reversed their roles; for in the earlier period the Court was identified as the protector of property rights and now it is regarded as the protector of human rights."[11]

Given the predicted changes in the Supreme Court under the Nixon administration toward a more conservative stance, we can expect another reversal of position toward the judicial process.

Inconsistencies have resulted from shifts in meaning of "liberal" and "conservative" to contrary positions. These inconsistencies have been hidden because these terms are used in such a loose and paradoxical manner that an individual may believe himself consistent as long as he continues to call himself "liberal" or "conservative."

Frequently, the inconsistency is in the method and not

the end. The consistency of end may account for shift in tactics or position when it appears that different circumstances require different and even opposite means for the same end. But when the methods used become identified with ends, or with "liberal" or "conservative" doctrine or ideology, ambiguity and confusion ensue.

Given difficulty in legislating unequivocal usage, it is better to drop these terms from discourse if only for the sake of clarity, consistency, fruitful dialogue, and resolutions of disputes. It would also apply to terms like "*status quo*," "change," "old," "new," "traditional," "modern," for none of these are inherently good or bad. Where they continue to be employed, no one should feel intimidated or reluctant to support policies however they may be described by these emotively and ambiguously loaded symbols.

Some, who have rejected being bound by the labels "liberalism" and "conservatism," merely consider whether changes would make things better or worse, and decide accordingly. Though they would tend to keep what is good, and change what is bad, they realize that even what is good might be changed for the better and what is bad might be changed for the worse.

"Change in itself tells us nothing of the character and consequences of the change desired—whether it is progressive or retrogressive, whether it furthers the interests of the entire community or of a portion of that community, and if a portion whether of the upper or middle or lower classes, or of the colored or white peoples, or of the urban or rural power groups, and so on. Clearly, it is in these things, not in the mere fact of change itself, that the true issues and divisions of political life reside."[12]

II. *What Price Revolution?*

Though America was born in revolution, contemporaries are surprised at the intensity with which it is being presently invoked even as a possibility. A few who are fed up with our current system are tempted by rebellion as the only feasible alternative to an "intolerable" state of affairs. They may feel encouraged and sanctified by historical rhetoric associated with the American Revolution and revered figures like Locke, Paine, and Jefferson.

At the eve of the American Revolution, Tom Paine proclaimed passionately in *Common Sense*:

> To talk of friendship with those in whom our reason forbids us to have faith, and our affections wounded thro' a thousand pores instruct us to detest, is madness and folly. Every day wears out the little remains of kindred between us and them; and can there be any reason to hope, that as the relationship expires, the affection will increase, or that we shall agree better when we have ten times more and greater concerns to quarrel over than ever?
>
> Ye that tell us of harmony and reconciliation, can ye restore to us the time that is past? Can ye give to prostitution its former innocence? Neither can ye reconcile Britain and America. The last cord now is broken, the people of England are presenting addresses against us. There are injuries which nature cannot forgive; she would cease to be nature if she did. As well can the lover forgive the ravisher of his mistress, as the Continent forgive the murders of Britain.[13]

If contemporary revolutionaries feel toward America the way Paine did toward Britain they will probably attempt revolution, however difficult. Many radicals not only speak with the same bitterness and hostility, but likewise foresee conditions deteriorating even more and despair of any reconciliation.

Over half a century before the American Revolution, an Englishman, John Locke, had asserted:

> Such revolutions happen not upon every little

mismanagement in public affairs. Great mistakes in the ruling part, many wrong and inconvenient laws, and all the slips of human frailty will be born by the people without mutiny or murmur. But if a long train of abuses, prevarications, and artifices, all tending the same way, make the design visible to the people, and they cannot but feel what they lie under and see whither they are going, it is not to be wondered that they should then rouse themselves and endeavor to put the rule into such hands which may secure to them the ends for which government was at first erected, and without which ancient names and specious forms are so far from being better that they are much worse than the state of nature or pure anarchy.[14]

It is significant that Locke refers to "the people" several times, as victims of abuse and instigators of rebellion. Revolutions are supposed to be made in the name of the people. Of course, it is possible to make a revolution "against" the people. If the people can replace one group and "put the rule into such hands which may secure to them the ends for which government was at first erected," the former rulers can attempt a counterrevolution to overthrow the new rulers who represent the people. That the former rulers are also "people" does not necessarily mean that their counterrevolution is one of "the people." Any group of individuals not representative of the people may rebel against a government representative of the people. Locke, then, was not defending revolution by people unless it was one made by "the people." That revolutions are made by "people" is a tautology; that they are made by "the people" is not. The distinction involves the difference between the few and the many, a minority and a majority. Thus not all revolutionaries or revolutions can invoke Locke's name in their support. In fact, some revolutionaries, if successful, would likely provoke Locke to support their overthrow, in the name of "the people."

The Declaration of Independence said: "Prudence, indeed, will dictate that governments long established should not be changed for light and transient causes; and accordingly all experience hath shown that mankind are more disposed to suffer while evils are sufferable, than to right themselves by abolishing the forms to which they are accustomed. But when a long train of abuses and usurpations pursuing invariably the same object, evinces a design to reduce them under absolute despotism, it is their right, it is their duty to throw off such government, and to provide new guards for their future security."[15]

The Declaration of Independence draws a distinction between mankind and government, and between governments characterized by absolute despotism and those that are not. The duty to overthrow government is reserved only for the former (despotism); not for "light and transient causes"; it is even better "to suffer while evils are sufferable." Those who invoke this document cannot do it cavalierly against any government; absolute despotism is a very extreme form which despotic governments may not reach. Contemporary revolutionaries would have quite a job on their hands to make a convincing case that the framers of the Declaration of Independence would have applied the phrase "absolute despotism" to recent America.

It is still understandable that Staughton Lynd should maintain:

"For almost two hundred years all kinds of American radicals have traced their intellectual origins to the Declaration of Independence and to the Revolution it justified. They have stubbornly refused to surrender the memory of the American Revolution to liberalism or reaction, insisting that only radicalism could make real the rhetoric of 1776."[16]

It turns out that conservatives, liberals, radicals, and revolutionaries trace back some of their ideas to the Declaration of Independence and the American Revolution. Conservatives invoke them as eternal truths, unchanging and revered traditions; liberals cite them as having provided us a flexible and workable framework for peaceful reform; radicals invoke them as justifying extreme and even violent acts for change; revolutionaries offer them justifying further revolutions. This is perhaps a greater tribute to the documents and historical events than to those who invoke them. On the other hand, it may be a greater tribute to the latter's ingenuity in interpreting ambiguous and abstract formulations and complex events in history in their own favor.

A number of revolutionaries are unwilling or unable to offer a substitute blueprint for the *status quo*, believing that their prime task is to tear down the "corrupt" and "illegitimate" institutions. Others have unclear notions of participatory democracy or a decentralized or even anarchistic society, but, in any case, one free of the evils of the present "racist," "imperialist," and "inegalitarian" system. Some believe or are disposed to gamble that revolution cannot make things worse, hoping that it will eventually improve conditions. If the "long run" is made long enough, let us say in twenty-five to fifty years, it is difficult to predict what will transpire; thus the more immediate dangers arising from revolution do not seem to weigh as heavily.

A cry for rebellion is often ambivalent; though sincere, it is intended to push the *status quo* in a direction which may make upheaval unnecessary. It offers the Establishment the option of either producing fundamental changes or facing continual confrontations culminating in revolt.

The revolutionary can cite concessions granted him as grounds for further threats to yield more concessions. Repressions which add to intolerable conditions can elicit additional justification for his tactics. Thus concessions or repressions increase the attraction of rebellion among the most militant. No doubt concessions or repressions reduce the appeal of revolt among less extreme elements.

In America, the public will favor repressions, particularly if convinced that concessions only lead to further demands. Is it possible to discourage revolution without excess repressions, and to alleviate social injustice without encouraging revolutionary blackmail?

However difficult it may appear at a moment of confrontation, at other times it should be possible to plan calmly and coolly to put down lawlessness and violence with minimum force, and to alleviate social injustice without encouraging revolution. It seems that exclusive use of either "carrot" or "stick" is not likely to be as successful as simultaneous or flexible employment of both. Continued and exclusive use of concessions, though winning some dissident support, will encourage more militant elements to increase their demands, threats, and violence. Continued and exclusive use of repression, though discouraging some militants, will encourage less militant elements to become more militant in the face of hopelessness about even token social reforms. Not every call for law and order and resistance to violence and revolution reflect opposition to reforms; not every call for alleviation of injustice and restraint by law enforcement agencies reflect contempt for law and order—though extremists may attempt to make it appear so. One must also expect certain extreme elements to act irrationally, whether in the name of law and order or revolution, regardless of what others may urge or do.

To quote an historic figure calling for rebellion (or anything else) presupposes that the original call not only was warranted, but is applicable to the contemporary scene. One can uphold the American Revolution and oppose a present one. It is possible to consider the American Revolution unjustified and yet urge one now. The chances of seizing power can make all the difference in the world in determining the soundness of an attempted rebellion, even if otherwise supportable.

Undoubtedly, "there has to be substantial evidence that a revolutionary situation is ripening. Ripeness means not only that the destructive aspects of the revolution will enjoy enough support to carry them out, but more importantly, that there are realistic prospects for introducing a better system."[17] One is reminded that, though the first American Revolution succeeded, the second American Revolution (Civil War) failed. There is the danger of plucking one's favorite examples from history, the "successful" rebellions, and ignoring the others. Two kinds of success are involved: one, subduing the old; the other, replacing it with something better. History offers little assurance that the first kind of success brings the second.

Can we say with much assurance that the American, French, or Russian revolutions were really successful in the second sense? The events may be too close to us emotionally because of upbringing and indoctrination, or too far away in space and time, to adequately reconstruct the conditions needed for objective assessment But we can try to judge anyway. In considering whether the new is better than the old, it is not merely a matter of simply comparing two different periods of time. One must consider the evils not only of the old but the new, not only during but after the revolution. In this regard, one can hardly paint a very favorable picture of the French and Russian revolutions, whatever one may think about the American Revolution. One rather misleading consideration is to credit the new regime with all the improvements without taking into account to what extent these would have occurred under the old regime. With this in mind, a close scrutiny of postrevolutionary America for about 100 years should be sufficient to indicate that the evil conditions of the old were not significantly improved by the new. Technological and scientific changes tend to affect all regimes regardless of ideology, though admittedly at different rates of change. Though some improvements have occurred and some evils have been reduced, the gap between the old and new is not as wide as it may appear. Some changes for the better would have probably occurred without revolution; the long-run consequences of a French Reign of Terror and the Napoleonic Era, the repressions and purges of a Lenin, Stalin, and Mao, need to be taken into account. Even in America, England had been making concessions to the colonies; the postrevolutionary gains hardly accrued to many, including the nonvoting whites and the enslaved blacks. History is not a convincing witness for the cause of revolution.

Even a handful can lead a revolt, but its chances of triumph are effected by widespread indifference and lack of opposition to it. However, it is not necessarily an overnight affair—historically it has frequently not been—it may be attempted piecemeal, over an indefinite period of time. It seems a feasible tactic in the United States, since the atmosphere is unsympathetic to revolution.

"It is obvious that nothing approaching the classic revolutionary situation exists in the United States today. The working-class, especially the organized working-class, is deeply committed to the *status quo* and has achieved substantial gains during the last thirty-five years; as a consequence, organized labor is a strongly anti-revolutionary force in the society. They and the middle-class (and the line separating them is often difficult to draw) have no desire to blow up the existing social system; indeed, if they confront efforts to bring about a revolution, they are likely to respond in a sharply negative fashion."[18]

Somewhat paradoxically, revolution may be pushed by "evolutionary" means, by more extreme forms of civil disobedience in which we find ourselves in a twilight area, not clear as to where civil disobedience ends and insurrection begins.

Unless convinced that conditions could not deteriorate even further, the revolutionary is playing a dangerous game; not only is he unlikely to win, but others will probably be encouraged to play the same game and transform the state of affairs into a nightmare. Theodore Draper, in recalling the role of the communists in pre-Nazi Germany and their fate after Hitler's seizure of power, points out:

"If a revolutionary minority strives to destroy a democratic, even a 'bourgeois-democratic,' order, is it necessarily going to be the main beneficiary—or even avoid the fate of the democratic order it has helped to pull down?"[19]

Recent developments in Indonesia attest to the dangers of the game of rebellion; communist revolutionaries had an important role in the Sukarno regime; fear of a Communist *coup d'état* contributed to an anticommunist, student-led revolution which turned into a bloodbath. Herbert Marcuse, generally sympathetic to student radicalism and rebellion, cites the Indonesian example as a counterrevolutionary tragedy:

"And one should never forget the one student rebellion which was instrumental in perpetrating the most despicable mass murder in the contemporary world: the massacre of hundreds of thousands of communists in Indonesia. The crime has not yet been punished; it is the only horrible exception from the libertarian, liberating function of student activism."[20]

Thus careful consideration is required of the assumptions that we are in the worst of all times, and revolution could not make things more horrible. Short of mass killing, torture or starvation, it is not easy to sustain such suppositions. In America, one can hardly uphold such assertions. Even if legal remedies and token progress were unavailable, there would be little logic in jumping from the frying pan into the fire. No doubt how one feels depends, in part, on where one finds oneself in the scheme of things. But how one feels is not a sufficient measure of whether things can become more dreadful. Even intolerable conditions can become more intolerable. Is it inconceivable for circumstances to become more unbearable for the millions who suffer from malnutrition, crowded ghetto conditions, illiteracy and racism? Wouldn't an unsuccessful revolution lead to a more oppressive state of affairs, even if a successful one did not? Is it not wise to consider the possibility of self-deception before it misleads one into regrettable and irreversible acts?

"Modern states are not so vulnerable to the Cohn-Bendits of this world as the dramatic nature of the barricades might make one suppose. Indeed, every fire lit in the streets is a vote cast for the right at the next election."[21]

One need only consider the response of local, state, and national authorities to rioting, looting, and campus seizures to conceive of the reception to anything resembling revolution. Legislation has been passed, and local, state, and national police and military forces have been trained and equipped; their excesses are condoned by the public.

In the United States, polarization has increased, the right gaining far more adherents than the left. It has occurred even without large-scale rebellion though, there have been civilly disobedient and violent acts and revolutionary threats on the left. The public fears, and not without reason, that a successful revolt, far from terminating violence, would provoke a continual series of violent and repressive acts. Once convinced that rebellious threats and violence will continue as long as the system is not abolished, the public may conclude that its only alternative is the cessation of concessions plus strong repressive steps. The battle cry will be that appeasement does not work, and law and order must be upheld.

"Past beneficiaries of New Left tactics have been Ronald Reagan, Richard Nixon and George Wallace, and they and other politicians should continue to ride the wave of reaction. Besides helping the Right, the New Left is also setting the stage for its own destruction. New Leftists have always had a greater appreciation for the present than the past, but they would do well to study the era of Joe McCarthy and other periods of political repression in America. The consequences of repression have never been revolution but rather the disintegration of the Left and a general curtailment of 'bourgeois' civil liberties."[22]

The most fruitful source of rebellion in America is the "black" problem, involving a sizable minority burdened with many injustices crying out for redress.

"Due to his semi-dependent status in society, the American Negro is the only potentially revolutionary force in the United States today."[23] But most blacks are not sold on the idea of revolution. The few who are have generally disavowed integration, thus alienating some who might otherwise cooperate with them. But even if blacks commonly supported revolution, a minority of 11 percent would face insuperable obstacles and mass repressions. Though the extent of racism, white and black, may have been exaggerated, it is sufficiently prevalent to arouse hysterical response to the slightest hint of a black revolution. This is already indicated by the public response to rioting, looting, and burning, acts which are far short of revolution.

"If large numbers of American Negroes insist on immediate satisfaction of all their just claims and righting of all past wrongs, on principle and without regard to the interests of other social groups, and on the threat of violence—that is, if Negroes are unwilling to submit their claims to the normal complex and nonprincipled compromises of the political process—a great many of our liberties are going to go by the board, and Americans are going to become familiar with all sorts of police state tactics that we have been fortunate enough to avoid in the past."[24]

Some revolutionaries conceive of a bloc of white and black radicals, aiming to build a broad coalition which can eventually hope for circumstances to arise where revolution might be feasible. Even if such a coalition could be formed and sustained, any attempt beyond the legal, political processes would be stopped in its tracks by local, state, and federal authorities with little inhibition by the public. This is already evident by reactions to groups like the Black Panthers and S.D.S.; by the growth of the Wallace movement in recent years, and the rise and growth of many right-wing groups, including the John Birch Society, the Minute men, and innumerable vigilante organizations throughout the land. There has also been a noticeable politicalization of police into pressure groups, offering themselves for public office and winning. The tragedy of the blacks is two-fold: they have suffered a great injustice; but in face of waves of repression, blacks, innocent as well as guilty, are not likely to be spared outbursts of fury and reaction, while white revolutionaries can, by mere change in attire and hair style, disappear into the white population. Ironically, the blacks have the greatest stake in preventing revolution, for they would be its greatest victims.

Many rebels recognize that their tactics have provoked in creased repressions and less reforms, but they believe these responses are insignificant. They feel that even without radical resistance and even with token reforms, our racist, materialist, imperialist, and militarist society would become progressively worse in the long run. Thus, ultimate overturn of the present system is a fundamental objective, the only hopeful alternative to a continually deteriorating state of affairs.

A few revolutionaries make much of the theory that things must get much worse before they can get much better, that greater repressions are necessary in order to radicalize large numbers of victims of repression; this will help to broaden the revolutionary base for ultimate overthrow of the Establishment. Of course, it is one thing for things to get worse without provocation or excesses by the revolutionaries. Here, there is some assurance that continued repressions would win public sympathy for the repressed and radicals. But if radicals threaten revolution and provoke more repression, the public and even victims of repression are likely to blame the radicals for worsening conditions; greater support, publicity, and propaganda in favor of repression is likely to come from the authorities and the public. One would have hoped that some would have learned from the rise of Hitler that things must get worse before they can become much worse, and that, if things become much worse, they can become still worse than that.

Some of our young revolutionaries may tell us that they welcome a "temporary" strengthening of reaction, since the far right will eliminate or weaken the social-democrats, liberals, and conservatives and thus sharply polarize society into two completely hostile segments, the forces of revolution and those of reaction, and that they will emerge victorious from this confrontation. Our response can only be that right-wing repression would destroy all that we value in American society, and that the ultimate victory of revolution over reaction in this country is just as unlikely as it was in Germany before Hitler, when the Communist Party defended its tactical alliances with the Nazis by the unrealistic argument that Fascism, having eliminated all the enemies of Communism, would prove unable to deal with the objective social problems, and that its collapse would permit the German Communist Party to emerge as the "residual legatee."[25]

If their projections of doom are correct, perhaps they have made a case, ironically, against revolution, civil disobedience, and reform at the present time. If they wait long enough for conditions to regress, without inciting fear of pending revolution, they may obtain greater support from more people, when revolutionary action may be more propitious. Reforms may interfere with such prospects by diverting or deluding the "victims" of society. Of course, revolutionaries cannot control the flow of reforms; they can discourage it by provoking reaction, but this might earn them more enemies than friends. Apparently, reforms should be made to appear token and useless without arousing a backlash.

What is "token" may be in the eyes of the beholder. The establishment is expected to blow up all improvements into changes of substance; but the revolutionary is prepared to do the opposite, deflate any reforms as token trivial and trite.

Proponents of reform admit it is inadequate but are unwilling to accept violence and rebellion, doubting they would produce a more desirable state of affairs. But whether reforms are adequate or merely "token" is an unclear, tricky and misleading question. There are diverse ways of evaluating "progress," arousing different psychological reactions. Measurements may be made by percentages or actual numbers, in the long run or short run, by comparison with prior periods or other groups or other countries, and so on. The results vary accordingly with significant differences in psychological impact.

For example, the condition of the most disadvantaged citizens, perceived in numbers involving millions, appears, deplorable, whereas, perceived in percentages of around 5 percent of the population, seems less discouraging. Comparing them with people of top or even average income reflects a very unsatisfactory plight, whereas comparing them with the disadvantaged over the past decades or centuries or in other parts of the world suggests a more hopeful status. For example:

"More educated Negroes hold executive jobs in major corporations and federal agencies than ever before, but the gap between white income and Negro income has almost doubled in the last twenty years. More suburban housing is available to Negroes, but housing conditions in the ghetto are steadily declining."[26]

But similar difficulties arise in perceiving the consequences of revolution. Do we count the oppressed or dead in millions, or by the percentage of population? Do we compare those on bottom, before and after revolution, or the gap between poor and rich, before and after revolution, and by numbers or percentages?

It is suggested that

there has to be a rough calculus of revolutionary violence. Before the resort to revolution is justifiable, there has to be good reason to believe that the costs in human suffering and degradation inherent in the continuation of the *status quo* really outweigh those to be incurred in the revolution and its aftermath. To put the point with appalling crudeness, one has to weigh the casualties of a reign of terror against those of allowing the prevailing situation to continue, which may include a high death rate due to disease, ignorance—or at the other end of the scale, failure to control the use of powerful technical devices. (The 40,000 deaths a year in the United States due to automobile accidents come to mind here. What would we think of a political regime that executed 40,000 people a year?)[27]

Whatever method may be used in calculating costs and gains, one would expect a consistent application in comparing the conditions of revolution and the *status quo*. Thus, outrage at the *status quo* by focusing exclusively on the number of deprived, even if only a small percentage of the total population, would likewise require that the casualties of revolution be similarly considered, even if only a small percentage of the total. Is the rebel unwilling to accept the suffering of a blameless few before, but not during and after, the revolution? Even Herbert Marcuse admits:

"However, the question cannot be brushed aside by saying that what matters today is the destruction of the old, of the powers that be, making way for the emergence of the new. Such an answer neglects the essential fact that the old is not simply bad, that it delivers the goods, and that people have a real stake in it. There can be societies which are much worse —there are such societies today. The system of corporate capitalism has the right to insist that those who work for its replacement justify their action."[28]

Those who believe that reforms are unsatisfactory because society is inherently "rotten" and that only by its overthrow can adequate changes be attained may find themselves in an embarrassing position. They may discover that the "rottenness" is not a monopoly of the particular society, but in fact characterizes any society, perhaps man himself. It is surely not too early to judge that so-called "socialist" systems suffer from "imperialist," "exploitative," "racist," bureaucratic, corruptive tendencies, just as the so-called capitalist societies do. They may learn that what they bought even in the long run was not worth the price. If the source of racism is to be found in human psychology as well as economic conditions, if imperialism and militarism are products of nationalism and international anarchy as well as economic greed and domination, if poverty and unemployment are rooted in overpopulation as well as insufficient economic planning, then revolution is hardly a panacea. A concerted effort to achieve world government and world population control would contribute far more to ameliorate these conditions than mere revolutionary changes in national governments.

Even if the present system is to blame, can the revolutionary demonstrate that his program outside the system will be more successful than reform within the system?

One may switch from arsenic, admittedly a cause of death, to cyanide, which is hardly an improvement. Just as death has different causes, societies' defects may have different causes; a system believed to cause defects may be replaced by an entirely different system leading to similar or even worse defects. Herbert Marcuse argues:

> Consequently, if the alternative is ruled by an elite, it would only mean replacement of the present ruling elite by another; and if this other should be the dreaded intellectual elite, it may not be less qualified and less threatening than the prevailing one. True, such government, initially, would not have the endorsement of the majority 'inherited" from the previous government—but once the chain of the past governments is broken, the majority would be in a state of flux, and, released from the past manager, free to judge the new government in terms of the new common interest. To be sure, this has never been the course of a revolution, but it is equally true that never before has a revolution occurred which had at its disposal the present achievements of productivity and technical progress. Of course, they could be effectively used for imposing another set of repressive controls, but our entire discussion was based on the proposition that the revolution would be liberating only if it were carried by the non-repressive forces stirring in the existing society. The proposition is no more—and no less— than a hope.[29]

Can he insure that power removed from the "exploiters" will end up in the hands of the "exploited" and remain there? The problems raised by revolution make the case for it difficult even in countries with more intolerable conditions than the United States. One who believes America is so inherently hopeless that even revolution is preferable is taking greater risks with revolution than with America.

It is argued that reforms under the present system have continued to be inadequate. But changes resulting from past revolutions have also continued to be inadequate, and at a much higher cost of suffering. If it is claimed that, whatever may have been the fate of past revolutions, they can hope to pull off a more successful one in the future, one can also hope that future reforms will be far better than past ones.

If past rebellions, including our own, have left much to be desired, then we may wonder if answers are to be found in this direction. Rather than seek revolutionary solutions, let them reconsider the possibilities of a reformist approach.

FOOTNOTES

1. See Dean Smith's *Conservatism* and Milton Viorst's *Liberalism* for recent statements of these positions.
2. David Spitz, "A Liberal Perspective on Liberalism and Conservatism," in *Left, Right and Center,* edited by Robert A. Goldwin, Rand McNally & Company, 1968, p. 20.
3. Frank S. Meyer, "Conservatism," in *ibid.,* p. 7.
4. M. Stanton Evans, *The Future of Conservatism,* Holt, Rinehart, and Winston, 1968, p. 12.
5. David Spitz, *op. cit.,* p. 25.
6. Henry Steele Commager, *Freedom and Order,* George Braziller, 1966, p. 11.
7. Frank S. Meyer, *op. cit.,* p. 8.
8. M. Stanton Evans, *op. cit.,* p. 91.
9. John P. Roche, *Courts and Rights: The American Judiciary in Action,* second edition, Random House, 1966, p. 116.
10. Martin Diamond, "Conservatives, Liberals, and the Constitution," in *Left, Right and Center,* p. 72.
11. David Spitz, *op. cit.,* p. 19.
12. *Ibid.,* pp. 21–22.

13. Howard Fast, *The Selected Works of Tom Paine and Citizen Tom Paine*, Modern Library, Random House, 1943, pp. 30–31.
14. John Locke, *The Second Treatise of Government*, Library of Liberal Arts, 1952, p. 126.
15. "The Declaration of Independence," in *Social and Political Philosophy*, edited by John Somerville and Ronald E. Santoni, Anchor Books, Doubleday & Co., 1963, p. 240.
16. Staughton Lynd, *Intellectual Origins of American Radicalism*, Pantheon Books, 1968, p. 7.
17. Barrington Moore, Jr., "Tolerance and the Scientific Outlook," in *A Critique of Pure Tolerance*, R. P. Wolff, B. Moore, Jr., H. Marcuse, Beacon Press, 1969, pp. 75-76.
18. Herbert A. Deane, "Reflections on Student Radicalism," in *Up Against the Ivy Wall*, edited by Robert Friedman, Atheneum, 1969, pp. 289–290.
19. Theodore Draper, "The Ghost of Social-Fascism," in *Commentary*, February 1969, Vol. 47, No. 2, p. 29.
20. Herbert Marcuse, *An Essay on Liberation*, Beacon Press, 1969, pp. 59–60.
21. Patrick Seale and Maureen McConville, *Red Flag/Black Flag: French Revolution, 1968*, G. P. Putnam's Sons, 1968, p. 234.
22. Carl Gershman, "Isolation of the New Left," in *Nation*, May 26, 1969, Vol. 208, No. 21, p. 668.
23. Harold Cruse, "Revolutionary Nationalism and the Afro-American," in *Black Fire*, Edited by Leroi Jones and Larry Neal, William Morrow & Company, Inc., 1968, p. 62.
24. Martin Shapiro, *Freedom of Speech: The Supreme Court and Judicial Review*, Prentice-Hall, 1966, p. 138.
25. Herbert A. Deane, *op. cit.*, p. 290.
26. Stokely Carmichael, "Toward Black Liberation," in *Black Fire*, pp. 128–129.
27. Barrington Moore, Jr., *op. cit.*, p. 76.
28. *Ibid.*, p. 86.
29. *Ibid.*, pp. 70–71.

CHAPTER V

THE COLD WAR IN THE NUCLEAR AGE

I. Democracy and Communism

The conflict between "democracy" and "communism" is perhaps the most significant confrontation pervading the contemporary world scene. Unfortunately, these emotionally charged terms are so ambiguous that discussions become impaled on the horns of semantic bewilderment. It is not clear whether we are talking about political systems, economic systems or a combination of the two. Some identify "democracy" with the economic system called "capitalism" while others equate "communism" with the economic system known as "socialism," thus attributing their defects and virtues to each other. Similar difficulties arise for those who identify them with the political systems of political democracy and totalitarianism. Understandably, the fact that we always experience political and economic systems as coexisting can account for part of the confusion. Some who grant the distinction maintain that they are so uniquely interrelated that they cannot or should not be considered independently.

"Economic relations and habits cannot be set apart in isolation any more than political institutions can be."[1] Do comparisons between alternative economic systems require a political framework and, conversely, do comparisons between different political systems require an economic framework? Are economies and governments of nations inseparable?

We can look at government in at least two distinct ways: its role in directing the economy, from one extreme of non-intervention to the other extreme of complete intervention, which reflects different economic systems, e.g., capitalism and socialism; the role of citizens in controlling the government, from one extreme of no voice to the other extreme of complete voice, which characterizes different political systems,

121

e.g., totalitarianism and democracy. Thus we can draw certain distinctions between economic and political systems though each involves the concept of government. Therefore, it should be possible to evaluate alternative economic systems without regard to political systems and vice versa.

That political and economic systems do not exist independently or are not found in practice to be separate does not mean that they cannot be thought of and evaluated independently. Even if the coexistence of political and economic systems were logically necessary, *i.e.*, they could not possibly exist independently, it would not prevent us from distinguishing them and evaluating them independently. Given the same political system, one can compare alternative economic systems; this can also be reversed in order to compare alternative political systems.

Is the copresence of political and economic systems logical, or merely factual or contingent? It seems that the existence of a political system logically entails the existence of an economic system, and conversely. But the existence of a particular type of political system does not logically entail the existence of a particular type of economic system, and conversely. Apparently a government presupposes a political and economic system, and conversely. It also appears that a society presupposes a government and conversely; thus a society presupposes an economic and political system, and conversely. But some anarchists may argue that government is not necessary for a political system, economic system, or society. They may be referring to a political system in which people and government coincide; the people have a complete voice in controlling the "government"; the economic system consists of nonintervention by government in the economy since there is no government apart from the people to intervene. On the other hand, there is perhaps no need to talk of government at all here; a political or economic system or a society could exist without "government." If one chooses to speak this way, then extreme anarchism can be described as an extreme form of democracy and an extreme form of capitalism. However unlikely this state of affairs may be, it is at least conceivable.

Whatever the relative merits of different economic systems, the crucial issue between democracy and communism is to be found in their political systems.

The basic issue "is whether human beings are to be entrusted with freedom of choice to determine their own governments, their own cultural outlook, and their own economic system, or whether it is to be chosen for them. Despite their campaigns of semantic corruption with such terms as "democracy and "freedom," the partisans of communist ideology have resolutely denied genuine liberty of choice to the people, first by the methods by which they seize power and even more by the methods by which they keep it. One can openly admit a multitude of evils, some of them shameful, in any existing democratic state, but so long as the processes of criticism, opposition, and education are not monopolized by a minority political party and supervised by a secret police, which is the case in every Communist state in the world, those evils are remediable."[2]

In this sense the conflict is between political democracy and totalitarianism. The same holds for the conflict between democracy and fascism. An undesirable economic system can be changed by the people in a country governed by them; this is not possible in one governed by a few. A desirable economic system is likely to be diverted to the benefit and purposes of those in power at the expense of the people in a society controlled by a few.

One measure of a desirable economic system is its economic growth. "No other test of social success has such nearly unanimous acceptance as the annual increase in the Gross National Product. And this is true of all countries developed or undeveloped; communist, socialist or capitalist."[3] Thus, however concerned we may be with the economic system, primary consideration should be directed toward the political system.

To argue that an economic system cannot be desirable

unless it is linked with a politically democratic system is to deal with a different question, namely, the virtues of a combined economic and political system. Perhaps it would be better to suggest that an economic system combined with a political democracy is better than that economic system combined with another political system. It is one thing to say that an economic system A combined with a political system B is undesirable. It is another thing to say that economic system A is undesirable because it is combined with political system B. It is useful to distinguish between the merits of a political system and an economic system. Otherwise we may attribute the merits of one to the other. Thus if we ask if a political system is desirable or better than another political system, we will find there are those who argue that no political system can be desirable, etc., unless it is linked with a particular economic system. We are back where we started, unwilling to make distinctions and unable to make separate evaluations. We need to point out that here also, one can say that a political system A combined with an economic system B is undesirable. But one ought not to express this by saying that political system A is undesirable because it is combined with economic system B.

Some believe that private enterprise is as important as political democracy for the preservation of freedom.

"The theory is that capitalism, interpreted as the maximum range of free personal opportunity for production and exchange of goods and services, is the Siamese twin of democracy. For the former is identical, so it is claimed, with the personal qualities of initiative, independence, vigor, that are the basic conditions of free political institutions. Hence, so it is argued, the check given to the operation of these personal qualities by governmental regulation of business activities is at the same time an attack upon the practical and moral conditions for the existence of political democracy."[4]

Once government achieves ownership or control of major industries, we are at the mercy of an all-powerful state able to coerce us into submission if we fail to do its bidding. Unless the individual has economic liberty, his political rights become virtually useless or impotent. However, even if political liberty cannot exist without economic liberty, can economic liberty exist for long without political liberty?

Others maintain that capitalism is incompatible with democracy, that socialism is a necessary condition for a democratic society. Lenin attacks capitalist democracy claiming that it is "always bound by the narrow framework of capitalist exploitation, and consequently always remains, in reality, a democracy for the minority, only for the possessing classes, only for the rich."[5] But similar characteristics could arise in a society which abolished private capitalism, where government officials, a new class, exploited the masses.

Defenders of capitalism or socialism must acknowledge the dangers of abuse and exploitation by individuals in business or government. Uncontrolled capitalism and uncontrolled socialism can be equally harmful to the interests and freedom of the average citizen. It turns out that mechanisms to prevent abuses in either economic system require the use of different institutions of government. Under capitalism this may include a variety of regulations culminating in something akin to the welfare state. Under socialism, this may involve separation of power and checks and balances in the management, production and distribution of goods and services. But in either case, whether industry is directed by individuals privately or in government, the total population must have the final say in order to prevent exploitation of the many by the few. Thus the political system becomes the crucial factor in the whole picture.

Though power emanates from many directions, its greatest source is found in government, since it commands the military and police forces. This is why defenders of capitalism and socialism are so concerned with the power of government and incorporate its role in describing their respective economic systems. But since the function of government is determined by those who control it, the nature of the political system is a key to the operation of the economic system.

It is in this sense that the political system is more significant than the economic system.

A capitalist proponent must admit that a government with complete dominion over life and death and freedom of thought is more dangerous than one which merely controls the economy. He may learn that whatever economic liberties he possesses under capitalism are useless in a society which represses and terrorizes its citizens. This is illustrated by countries like Spain, Portugal, and South Africa. A socialist must acknowledge that a government with complete power over the economic and military resources is better able than private capital to exploit the masses. He may discover that he has replaced one set of exploiters (capitalists) with another in a socialist state which is politically totalitarian. This is exemplified by Russia, Mainland China, and most of Eastern Europe.

Marx and Engels, in "The Communist Manifesto," insisted on the necessity of raising "the proletariat to the position of ruling class, to establish democracy."[6] They recognized that unless the state was directed by the "proletariat," socialism as they conceived it could not be achieved. Mere ownership of the means of production would not guarantee that the state was controlled by the proletariat.

If socialist and capitalist proponents who believe in political democracy grant that their common political values are more significant than their economic differences, they will join together in resisting the totalitarian call of those who appear to share their economic views.

It should be granted that whatever inequitable influence private wealth has in a capitalist society, the presence of political democracy can make a significant difference in offsetting this; this is surely reflected in legislation associated with the welfare state and can be expected to continue indefinitely with greater reforms. It should also be recognized that, whatever corruption, inefficiency, and monopoly government ownership of industry may bring, political democracy can play an important role in curbing this; this is demonstrated by revisions and reversals of socialist trends and by election of more conservative parties in England and the Scandinavian countries.

Some attach great importance to whether major industries are owned privately or by government, but this difference may be overrated. In a capitalist society with sufficient government regulation, or in a socialist society with sufficient material incentives, the distinction between private and government ownership may be of little substance.

Either private individuals or the government has title to a company; either private stockholders collect dividends and interest or government employees collect wages and commissions; either people turn over part of their profits through taxes to government or government receives income directly from business and subsequently distributes part of it as salaries and bonuses; either the private owner or the manager of a publicly owned steel plant bribes a tax collector; these may turn out to be the same in content however different in form. Different capitalist societies vary in the balance between individual rights and public needs, and the same applies to socialist countries; thus similar states of affairs are described in different terms and similar ideologies cover contrasting conditions.

It is amusing to hear capitalist spokesmen condemn programs involving government ownership and regulation as socialist, but praise the armed forces, public education, federal programs for interplanetary flight, subsidies, and pollution control. It is similarly ironic to hear socialist leaders condemn suggestions for profit incentive and private enterprise as revisionist and bourgeois, while they support material incentives for scientists and artists to encourage greater achievement and output.

In the United States, "The services of Federal, state, and local governments now account for between a fifth and a quarter of all economic activity. In 1929 it was about eight percent. This far exceeds the government share in such an avowedly socialist state as India, considerably exceeds that in the anciently social democratic kingdoms of Sweden and Nor-

way, and is not wholly incommensurate with the share in
Poland, a Communist country which, however, is heavily agri-
cultural and which has left its agriculture in private ownership."[7]

In either case, the government can do whatever is necessary for the public good, or fail to do this; neither private
nor government ownership possesses inherent superiority or
inferiority in these matters.

No doubt ideological extremists on both sides will flinch
at the use of the terms "capitalist" or "socialist" for such
models. Some capitalist advocates may call it socialist and
some socialists may return the compliment by calling it capitalist, each group perhaps considering it a sell-out to the
other. These purists not only disagree verbally about the use
of the terms "capitalist" and "socialist," but differ considerably about the roles of government and incentive in the economic system. But the "moderates" in both camps who recognize that both government and material incentives have
important functions in the good society may come to realize
that they are much closer than their favorite ideological vo-
cabulary suggests.

Some defenders of capitalism see the struggle between
"democracy" and "communism" as one primarily between ad-
verse economic systems. Believing that the economic system
has priority over the political system, they are tempted to
aid capitalist nations even if totalitarian and are reluctant to
support socialist nations even if politically democratic. Is it
tenable to support totalitarian capitalist countries because
they are capitalist? Ironically, some of the fears capitalist
spokesmen express of socialism reflect evils associated with
totalitarian governments, where the state has complete power
with no recourse by the individual against the government.
To believe that capitalism can be preserved and flourish in a
totalitarian state is to expect too much of humans with great
power. Would withholding aid from political democracies
which are not capitalist be effective in moving their economies toward capitalism?

Most communist governments, despite their internal differences, are opposed to both political democracy and capitalism throughout the world. They fear that a politically democratic nation, even if socialist-oriented, may restore capitalism. They also dread the challenge of political freedom to their one-party totalitarian structure. Recent attempts by Czechoslovakian communists to democratize politically have been met by Soviet intervention and occupation. This reflects, in part, anxiety by orthodox communists toward the spread of political freedom and capitalism in Eastern Europe and the Soviet Union. Therefore, it appears to be to the interest of those who oppose communism on economic grounds to support political democracies, whatever their economic structure. However distasteful one fancies a socialist economy to be, it is more desirable under democratic than communist auspices.

Those who conceive the struggle between democracy and communism to be primarily political, may be reluctant to aid totalitarian countries even if not under communist sway. Concerned with the defense of political democracy, they may consider a noncommunist dictatorship as undesirable as a communist one, and thus no more deserving of support. Their attitude is similar to those who consider a socialist economy, whether in a democratic or communist society, equally dangerous. But they are equally mistaken. Most communist regimes are interested in overthrowing not only capitalism and political democracy, but also any government not under communist dominion. In fact, some communist regimes support removal of leaders or factions of other communist regimes not in sympathy with their own "brand" of communism. This is reflected especially in the Sino-Soviet conflict. At the present time therefore a dictatorship appears to be less dangerous under noncommunist than communist control. There is greater opportunity, generally, to encourage political freedom in a noncommunist country than a communist one, since the latter is part of a large bloc unsympathetic to political democracy. Even where opportunity for freedom is lacking, it seems less dangerous than an enlarged communist bloc. This is in sharp contrast with the 1930s and 1940s when the fascist bloc was on the rise and constituted a greater menace than the communists. At present it seems feasible to give aid to noncommunist regimes regardless of their political or economic systems, in order to contain the spread of communist totalitarianism.

> Where political aid is needed, and many years' time for growth of political maturity on the part of a people, it is quite foolish to demand democratic expression of a people's will before there can be legitimacy in the government to be aided. If, in such a situation, intervention may often be immoral and unfeasible, nonintervention may also immorally abandon a people, and tragically may be no more effective in accomplishing what politically ought to be done. This describes the situation in which the leaders of a great power must determine how best to use power commensurate with the responsibilities that have devolved upon us in the present age.[8]

But simply giving aid is insufficient. There are economic, political, military, and psychological factors to be taken into account. In countries containing pockets of economic discontent and impoverishment, fertile grounds exist for planting seeds of violence and revolutionary agitation. Parts of South America and Africa appear vulnerable in this respect. Economic reform is essential to avoid being confronted with the rise of communist movements attempting to establish a foothold for insurrection and wars of liberation.

"Earlier land reforms seem to lessen the appeal of guerrillas to the Bolivian peasant just as, first in the 1870s and then again under General MacArthur, they have stabilized and enriched the Japanese countryside."[9]

In some cases, the undemocratic political structure diverts economic aid from the needy into the hands of the ruling powers. This may necessitate encouragement of political and social reforms as conditions for economic aid in order that it benefit those most susceptible to communist appeals. The point is that we cannot assume that support without strings attached will always succeed. It may have the opposite effect if it strengthens the few on top and thereby widens the gap between the have and have-nots.

"We will help the poor, the disadvantaged, the distressed where our help can do some good, where our aid can get directly to the people we want to help. But we will not pour billions into the hands of corrupt rulers and fascistic dictators in the misguided belief that we are purchasing friends for the 'free world.' "[10]

In some countries conditions may have gone beyond the point where economic aid or political reform would be sufficient, necessitating military support to prevent a communist take-over through wars of liberation or *coup d'états*. Viet Nam seems to represent such a case prior to massive American military intervention during the period 1965 to 1968.

There are two assumptions to be avoided here. One is that economic and political reforms will always be sufficient to contain communism; the other, that military aid will always be enough to accomplish the task. Too often recommendations are made on a basis of what might have been appropriate earlier. Even if communist strength has grown as a result of deplorable economic and political conditions, reform by itself may not do the job at a later date, particularly where communist forces have begun guerrilla or other forms of military action. But military aid by itself may be insufficient and continued economic and political reform may be necessary. Again, Viet Nam is an appropriate example of these kinds of circumstances.

Aid may be met with hostility from recipient countries as a result of pride, nationalism, or other reasons. But automatic refusal to help except on our own terms may encourage greater resentment and communist exploitation of disunity and divisiveness. The policy of support needs to be sufficiently flexible so that common goals are not submerged by differences.

The communist bloc is also characterized by disagreements and disunity. Aid should be extended in order to exploit their internal differences. Flexibility is also essential in dealing with economic, political, and psychological factors. Among their divisive issues is the desire for economic progress and national independence. This provides opportunity to encourage trade agreements and cultural exchanges which promote more peaceful and democratic tendencies among the communist nations. Fear of "aiding our enemies" assumes that they benefit more than we do from interaction. But if we cut off commerce with our allies it would harm us in many different ways; the communist bloc can obtain our goods by trading with our allies anyway. Even if we were somehow able to persuade the rest of the world not to trade with the communist countries, they are unlikely to collapse; they would probably be welded into a more unified bloc economically, politically, and militarily. In the long run, more significant than exchange of goods is exchange of ideas. In our own society, there is a much greater flow of ideas from all sources, democratic, communist, and so on, than in the communist nations; thus, cultural, scientific, and intellectual exchange should spread our own democratic values more than their totalitarian ones.

Nationalism and ideological differences open avenues for weakening ties that bind them into a unified world bloc. There is evidence that "in a world where nationalism remains a force of tremendous strength, an internationalist doctrine is bound to come into conflict with the interests of any major communist power or with the desire of smaller Communist states for autonomy."[11]

Recent negative responses from many communist parties and countries to Soviet intervention in Czechoslovakia and to the doctrine of "limited sovereignty" are barometers of the distance traveled from the once highly unified and monolithic communist bloc. It should be easier to contain a communist world no longer monolithic since their differences will impede their cooperation in support of communist expansion.

However, one may overstate their divisions and misread

the effect of discord on their common aims. Some of their disputes have promoted rivalry in giving economic and military aid to their allies; competition between Russia and China in aiding North Viet Nam indicates they have not given up the goal of spreading communism. That communist governments resist domination by other communist governments does not prevent them from encouraging communism in other countries.

"If the behavior of the North Vietnamese regime is any indication—in Laos as well as South Viet Nam—there is little cause for regarding the emergence of Titoist regimes as an occasion for relaxation and good cheer."[12]

Much has been made of economic divergences among communist countries and particularly moves by some toward limited capitalism. Though this has the advantage of promoting differences among them, it has encouraged unwarranted assumptions about the conflict between democracy and communism. As pointed out earlier, some interpret it in terms of economic systems, *i.e.*, between capitalism and socialism. Therefore, they see capitalist tendencies as a sign of success for "democracy" over "communism." Any development, whether capitalist or otherwise, that abets dissension in the communist bloc, aids democracy to the extent that it impedes communist expansion. But this does not mean that political democracy has obtained a foothold within the communist countries. We recall that in the 1920s Lenin adopted a limited form of capitalism under the N.E.P. program. Totalitarianism is compatible with a variety of economic systems, from socialism to capitalism, from the Soviet Union to Franco Spain.

We are reminded that the political system deserves priority, and the value of the economy depends on who controls the government. We also need to be wary of relaxation in censorship and expression of unorthodox ideas. Too frequently, they are temporary and subject to the wishes of a handful of powerful leaders in the Communist Party. Though the communist nations have moved significantly from the period of "Stalinism," they have a long distance to go before one can describe them in democratic terms; the hopeful signs in Czechoslovakia, followed by its repression, are grim reminders of the long road ahead. The communist nations, regardless of economic and other modifications, will continue to be a danger and need to be contained as long as they support political totalitarianism internally and externally.

II. *War and Peace*

The quest for peace on earth cannot be pursued in the abstract. We need to inquire into specific conditions, including the nature of man, diverse political and economic systems, ideologies, military power and international relations. Human beings are committed not only to peace but political and economic values, religious and cultural beliefs and different ways of life.

Are we concerned with peace in the short run or the long run and what is their relationship? It is understandable that individuals should risk future evils to avoid present suffering and death. But future generations might condemn the present one for not preventing evils they may inherit as a consequence. It is ironic to find members of the present generation unwilling to suffer for the future, yet condemning past generations for having done the same. Is it sometimes necessary to give up peace temporarily in order to assure it in the long run? Or do wars produce more wars, so that we are better off grasping at peace immediately at whatever price? Is the value of peace higher than any other value, including freedom? Would our refusal to fight under any circumstances encourage others to be peaceful or would it embolden belligerence? Would pacifism mean complete surrender, for example, to the Russians? Would it assure tranquility, or would the Russians use us in a conflict with the Chinese? Would we then have neither peace nor freedom?

"It is not simply that peace is a 'process,' a process that sometimes involves resort to arms. That seems too stark a paradox. Peace is not the only political good. It is rather that peace with justice and an ordered liberty is a 'process,' a process that sometimes involves resort to nonpeaceful means. It is not at all paradoxical that *this* should be the nature of international politics."[13]

The nuclear age has transformed the condition of man, requiring a radical revaluation of the options and methods of war and peace. The widespread destruction of World War II did not portend an end to most of the participating countries, let alone mankind. Even an act so generally condemned as preventive war might have been plausible in some circumstances in the prenuclear period.

But if a preventive nuclear war to preserve our way of life produced our own destruction, it would be self-defeating.[14] This suggests that we never initiate a nuclear conflict, and that we support the transfer of all nuclear weapons to an international authority, so that no nation can employ them.

"All nations would have to agree to reduce national armed forces to the level necessary for internal police action. No nation should be allowed to retain nuclear weapons or any other means of wholesale destruction."[15]

Is American unilateral disarmament feasible? Would it lead to the following? "It is probable that other heavily armed powers would follow the lead of this country and we would have a competition in disarmament rather than competition in armaments."[16] One does not have to treat all governments as aggressive. One may even consider the possibility that most nations would reciprocate in disarmament. But one strong country taking advantage of this situation could dominate the world militarily or even unleash a large-scale attack. It appears reasonable that unilateral disarmament should be shunned to discourage others from aggression or starting a nuclear war. This must be distinguished from unilateral "initiatives" taken to encourage bilateral or multilateral (general) disarmament or reduction of arms, in which further acts depend on the responses of others and thus does not leave one at their mercy.

What about our response to a nuclear assault? Clearly the

purpose of nuclear power is to offer the "adversary the prospect that any attack by his strategic forces would be met by a counterblow so devastating as to convert a decision to attack into a suicide pact."[17] Even though nuclear reprisal would complete the "suicide pact," we have to be prepared to retaliate, since doubts about our response could provoke a nuclear attack.

Aggression should be resisted by limited conventional power in order to avoid the awesome dilemma of nuclear war or complete surrender.

"Moreover, if we stand against all war in the nuclear age (and are not citizens of some lesser and non-nuclear power), this should be done in clear recognition of the fact that (if ours is more than a witnessing action and has any effect) our words and action will tend to make it more likely that the United States will use nuclear weapons *first* in some future encounter of power, since we would be undertaking to weaken our nation's resolve to provide itself with sufficient conventional strength and graduated and flexible response below the nuclear level. The way to be a *nuclear pacifist* and at the same time politically responsible would be precisely to stand *for* the possible justice of non-nuclear war today, and to foster and strengthen the means for conducting such a war successfully without resort to nuclear weapons (planning to surrender rather than go to nuclears)."[18]

The doctrine of massive retaliation is as self-defeating as preventive nuclear war; as Kissinger suggests, it "requires us in every crisis to stake our survival on the credibility of a threat which we will be increasingly reluctant to implement and which, if implemented, will force us into the kind of war our strategy should make every attempt to avoid."[19] A restrained military stand against totalitarianism increases the likelihood of preserving freedom and preventing nuclear disaster. The nuclear age has transformed the strategy and tactics of dealing with totalitarianism. It cannot be treated as it was in the past. If we try to attain complete victory, we invite all-out nuclear war since both sides will combat total defeat.

Paul Ramsey states that "the use of force has multiple consequences which must be weighed against one another —leading to the conclusion that it is wrong to engage in a war, however just in itself, if this leads to greater evil. This is the doctrine of coexistence, and it can happen that, in the nuclear age, this *jus contra bellum* will provide the basis for new institutions with worldwide powers. If so, this will be not so much because mankind's 'justices' became one, but because the common principle of expediency or proportionality in the use of power requires it, in order for violent means to be subdued and connected again with minimal political goals. This test seems apt to make 'nuclear pacifists' of us all." But, Ramsey goes on to say: "At the same time however, it has to be noted that those whose method of war is 'revolutionary' war, or insurgency or subconventional war, have to date no sufficient reason for believing that *these* 'just wars' may finally be unjustified because resorting to violence even in just insurgency causes is likely to lead to greater evil. Insurgency war has not been 'deterred' as generally as nuclear war. *Therefore* there is no 'coexistence' at this level."[20]

Though fear of nuclear war will not eliminate resort to revolutions and counterrevolutions, the nuclear powers are reluctant to allow unconventional type warfare to escalate into larger military conflict; but they may push its use as far as they can, hoping to be able to draw back in time. Cuba, West Berlin, the Southeast, and the Mideast, indicate the levels of risk in keeping the fires burning without blowing up the works. It also illustrates the dangers in using the rhetoric of "victory" and "defeat" of the prenuclear age.

The present goal must be restricted to stalemate and containment, not conquest or subjugation. Stalemate makes a negotiated settlement more acceptable by minimizing risk of loss of face and way of life.

The ideal situation would consist of world government with sufficient power to resolve disputes and prevent war. We realize that

this is a world in which the writ of United Nations

intervention would have to extend further than it has in the past if ever a policy of non-intervention in the affairs of other states is to become the single duty of the leaders of the member states, especially the leaders of a nation that has inherited power and responsibility in imperial (if still gravely limited) proportions. The right and duty of intervention can be morally and politically withdrawn from nation-states no more rapidly than this same right and duty is perfected in its exercise by world or regional public authorities. These are two ends of the same seesaw. There is an inverse logical and actual connection between having intervention thrust upon us —sometimes as a responsibility, always as a possibility— and being deprived of any such legitimate option by superior political authority. One good reason for correcting the structural defects of the nation-state system is precisely to avoid having intervention thrust upon us.[21]

There would still be the possibility of civil wars, rebellions, and conflicts among nations, but the power and need to wage war would be reduced and would thus contribute to a more peaceful world. The loss in sovereign power would be worth the gain in reducing the chances of a nuclear holocaust. However, the likelihood of nations surrendering their military forces to a world government appears extremely doubtful. Kissinger, highly skeptical about disarmament schemes, points out that "No reduction of forces, however scrupulously carried out, could protect the powers against a technological breakthrough. Even were strategic striking forces kept at fixed levels rigidly controlled, an advance in air defense sufficient to contain the opposing retaliatory force would upset the strategic balance completely."[22]

No doubt, no system could guarantee against a technological breakthrough, but it could reduce its probabilities, and thus be better than no controls. Regulated disarmament would also reduce the armaments race and make enforcement of world law more effective. But the difficulties with the United Nations, a far cry from world government, indicates that the latter is not likely to be forthcoming in the near future.

In the absence of world government, we are required to deal with threats to freedom in concert with other nations where possible and individually where necessary. But even in acting on our own, we are obligated to encourage the maximum use of international machinery in order to promote world law and world government. At present this means the United Nations. We must avoid the vicious cycle of nations acting on their own because there is no world government, and then finding there is no world government because nations act on their own. A major threat to freedom has been the spread of communist totalitarianism by means of wars of liberation. Unwillingness to withstand its expansion would encourage more communist civil wars and also tempt others to engage in aggressive policies

When the security and order of the world depends on arsenals of *militarily* useless weapons (nuclears whose use is their deterrent non-use), you can be sure that insurgency, subversion, and disorder can win victories with meager weapons that have at least this virtue, namely, that they can be used in support of somebody's purpose or policies. Thus, at the heart of the great strength of the modern state there is weakness (as Mao Tse-tung, Ho Chi Minh, General Nguyen Giap, and Che Guevara discerned). And in the weakness of the present guerrilla there is strength: better to strike and run away, and live to fight another day; and if there are enough of him who endure long enough they may bring down a whole nation without ever winning a conventional battle. This will remain the military situation for decades to come."[23]

Some have challenged the domino theory that resistance prevents further attacks since they have recurred anyway. But resistance cannot assure that no attacks will occur, only that fewer will take place, and, if they do, will be less likely to succeed. Others have argued that resistance applies to acts of aggression, not wars of liberation which differ essentially from attacks by one country upon another. They claim that wars of liberation are revolutions or civil wars which should be settled by indigenous elements of the country, not by external intervention. It is not suggested that every civil war, revolution or "war of liberation" is communist-led or communist-inspired. One must be as wary of those who describe all revolutionary movements as communist as those who describe communist movements as merely revolutionary. But subjugation is not confined to sending military forces across a border. It may also result from external aid to internal guerrilla activities and rebellions. If the reasons which justify intervention in another nation's foreign affairs also apply to a nation's internal affairs, then intervention may also be justified in the latter case. Wars of liberation play a significant role in advancing the system of the communist bloc throughout the world. They spread totalitarianism and thus constitute a threat to freedom comparable to attacks upon one country by another. Whether the forces are primarily native or foreign does not dispel the extension of totalitarianism. This was true of attempts in Greece after World War II, in Castro's Cuba, and in North and South Viet Nam. Aid to a country resisting aggression constitutes intervention in another nation's affairs. Thus the doctrine of nonintervention is not an unqualified principle. Whether intervention is justified depends on particular circumstances. Though American intervention to stop communist totalitarianism did not seem applicable to the Dominican Republic, it did seem appropriate in Castro's Cuba and Viet Nam.

There is a temptation to escalate limited wars in the hope that the other side will find the cost too high. Herman Kahn calls this theory, as reflected in the Viet Nam War, the assumption that "as soon as we show the North Vietnamese they cannot win, they will quit."[24] But this may trigger mutual escalation into a larger and even nuclear conflict. Even clashes between non-nuclear powers can escalate into conflicts involving the interests of the nuclear powers and thus risk nuclear war. This has been true in Cyprus, the Mideast, and the Congo. Even if a war continues indefinitely, restraint entails less danger than widening the conflict. Effort should be made to prevent defeat without spreading hostilities. The Korean conflict seemed to fit this pattern quite well.

Some may urge unilateral deescalation in order to evoke similar response by our adversaries, reduce the number of casualties, and increase chances of negotiation. It would be desirable, of course, if the other side were willing to negotiate and accept terms wherein they gained no territory. We could always turn down territorial demands and reverse deescalation if they refused to negotiate. But our deescalation may increase their reluctance to bargain and military strength. If they are indisposed to negotiate on terms acceptable to us, we can expect a similar response to deescalation, plus our military disadvantage. If they are inclined to bargain on acceptable terms, it ought to be attainable without deescalation, as long as we also refrain from escalating. If we deescalate while they increase or even maintain their military level, it will fortify their belief in victory, make them less minded to negotiate except on terms favorable to them, and improve their military position. Some feel that partial territorial concession may be feasible if only to end war. But even limited territorial gain would embolden further similar attempts, encourage potential victims to make accommodations and capitulate to the other side.

Of course, one must distinguish between unilateral and bilateral deescalation, the latter being feasible in a mutual and balanced reduction of hostilities. Even unilateral "initiatives" involving deescalation may be warranted if carried out on a small enough scale with careful safeguards to promptly reverse the process if there is lack of response on the other side.

One must also distinguish between one-sided territorial concessions and mutual ones which promote settlement on acceptable terms.

Resistance in another place might have been easier if we had not been menaced in the present locale. Some have suggested that Viet Nam was the wrong place for the United States to take a firm stand. But declining to meet the threat we are in fact facing would render opposition elsewhere more difficult. Those who suggest that we can take a stand later on if necessary are ignoring the psychological, military, and economic gain the other side will have attained by our unwillingness to stand firm at present. Furthermore, our adversaries are not likely to engage us in spots tailored to our convenience and interest.

Is there a limit to the blood and resources we are willing to expend to secure our allies? If their safety would ultimately affect ours, then the question becomes: what price are we prepared to pay to protect our own invulnerability? Some would bear any sacrifice, including nuclear war. Others believe that any military action exceeds acceptable bounds. This seems plausible where our own security is not connected with that of our allies.

Robert L. Heilbroner speculates:

> Suppose that most of Southeast Asia and much of Latin America were to go Communist, or to become controlled by revolutionary governments that espoused collectivist ideologies and vented extreme anti-American sentiments. Would this constitute a mortal threat to the United States?
>
> I think it fair to claim that the purely *military* danger posed by such an eventuality would be slight. Given the present and prospective capabilities of the backward world, the addition of hundreds of millions of citizens to the potential armies of communism would mean nothing when there was no way of deploying them against us. The prospect of an

invasion by Communist hordes—the specter that frightened Europe after World War II with some (although retrospectively, not too much) realism— would be no more than a phantasm when applied to Asia or South America or Africa.[25]

A little later on, Heilbroner goes on to say:

A world in which Communist governments were engaged in the enormous task of trying to modernize the worst areas of Asia, Latin America, and Africa would be a world in which sharp differences of national interest were certain to arise within these continental areas. The outlook would be for frictions and conflicts to develop among Communist nations with equal frequency as they developed between those nations and their non-Communist neighbors. A long period of jockeying for power and command over resources, rather than anything like a unified sharing of power and resources, seems unavoidable in the developing continents. This would not preclude a continuous barrage of anti-American propaganda, but it would certainly impede a movement to exert a coordinated Communist influence over these areas.[26]

It is interesting to find Heilbroner suggesting that there would be "no way of deploying" enemy forces against the United States. They could be landed by sea and air power, and from the countries North and South of continental United States. Also, indigenous elements could initiate guerrilla warfare and establish bases of operations for bringing outside enemy forces into the country. If this seems rather remote and unlikely it is because most parts of the underdeveloped lands are not yet under communist domination.

Heilbroner makes much of differences likely to arise among communist countries, conflicts involving national and economic interests, which "would certainly impede a movement to exert a coordinated Communist influence over these areas." As if differences between Hitler, Mussolini, and Hirohito prevented them from conducting a devastating war; as if differences between the United States and Russia prevented them from carrying on a war to victory against Hitler and his allies! As if differences between Russia and China prevented them from giving significant support to the Vietnamese communists, both in the 1950s and the 1960s! No doubt these alliances were impeded by differences; this is true of all alliances; but the question is whether they were *prevented* from attaining their common goals by their differences.

Even if Heilbroner were correct, what would be its effect on the people and governments of Europe and the United States, in resisting domestic and foreign communist pressures for accommodation, domination, and surrender? Nuclear power would be useless because of mutual overkill; granted differences among the communist bloc, in the long run conventional manpower and resources would be heavily weighted on their side; it would thus tempt them to support domestic and border insurrections, guerrilla warfare, blockade and economic warfare against the United States and her remaining allies. Would any burden short of nuclear war be excessive to insure our own freedom and security? If there is wider communist penetration of Asia, South America and Africa and command of their manpower and resources, what price might we then be required to pay to meet the forces aligned against us?

Even if such a fate were to befall us, if we were encircled by a totalitarian bloc, all might not be lost. We could by extreme measures hold onto our freedom and independence, and hope that in time changes might occur which would remove the outside threat. But to what extent would we be required to marshal our own manpower and resources to protect our shores from external and internal dangers? The imbalance in conventional manpower and resources might tempt either side to engage in preventive nuclear war. We might, in desperation, lacking conventional means to avert ultimate defeat. With worldwide land, manpower, and resources, the other side might be tempted, hoping they could survive a retaliatory response while we would succumb to a first-strike attack. This sounds nightmarish and fantastic, since we do not expect America to withdraw into isolationism, betray her allies, and allow most of the globe to fall under communist domination.

If we can protect our allies without raising our commitments, all well and good. If our opponents increase their level only if we do, then there is no point in lifting ours. But if they enlarge their help even if we do not, we may have to match their increase to avert defeat.

One alternative to military support wherever threats arise is selective commitment which minimizes sacrifice of lives and resources. It is suggested that only where governments and people have sufficient unity and strength can we hope to triumph in the long run. "The most decisive lesson of Viet Nam would seem to be that, no matter how much force it may expend, the United States cannot ensure the security of a country whose government is unable to mobilize and maintain sufficient popular support to control domestic insurgency."[27] But what we save in resources may be exceeded by what our adversaries gain in localities we have abandoned; thus, in a later confrontation we may be comparatively weaker. On the other hand, our support of a country in need of aid may be greeted with such an intensity of opposition from that country, from our allies or within our nation, that commitment would be more costly than profitable. Perhaps it is possible to render aid and yet hold dissension within manageable bounds, by convincing our own people, our allies, and those vulnerable to attack that it is in our interest to withstand our adversaries' domination and expansion.

Critics may raise sound questions about the nature and degree rather than the mere fact of commitment. We may support elements so oppressive that we inadvertently help rather than hinder our adversaries' attempt to recruit adherents.

"The United States poured money, manpower, and military hardware into the poor and unstable countries of the world so long as they professed to be anti-Communist. It justified alignment with any dictatorial, totalitarian, anti-democratic—even corrupt—regime of dubious color so long as it was not Red."[28] Or we may exceed the minimum required to achieve our goal in a wider and more costly military conflict. Or we may emphasize our own unilateral action rather than collective action and greater participation of others. American policy in Viet Nam has reflected some of these errors, particularly bombing of the North, Americanizing of the war and support of undemocratic forces in the South. The halt to the bombing of the North in 1968 and subsequent de-Americanizing and reduction of hostilities has not weakened the American overall position in resisting communist expansion in Southeast Asia. Although it is not always possible to satisfy criticism, it is not necessarily an abdication of responsibility; it may reflect a search for more effective programs.

The plausibility of selective support stems from its effort to predict self-defeating involvements. It appeals to the objectives of unrestricted support by attempting to avoid possible failure. But the unreliability of predictions suggests that it is safer to initially render aid in doubtful cases and subsequently reverse it if evidence warrants it. Reliance on past experience does not require abstention unless we have good reason to suspect that it is self-defeating.

Reversing or even revising a commitment raises dangers analogous to those resulting from refusing support; it reassures our adversaries and disheartens those in need of help. It is difficult in general to estimate which policy is less undesirable. But if the need to reassess does arise, there are options open short of the unpalatable choice of withdrawing support. We can still call upon our internal resources, those of our allies, those under direct attack by our adversaries, and whatever international structures exist for equitable resolution of the conflict. In the long run, it seems that over-commitment is preferable to undercommitment where evidence for and against support is not clear. In the nuclear age, in a lawless world, an ounce of conventional prevention is worth a pound of nuclear cure.

FOOTNOTES

1. John Dewey, *Freedom and Culture*, Capricorn Books, 1963, p. 9.
2. Sidney Hook, *Political Power and Personal Freedom*, Collier Books, 1962, p. 158.
3. John K. Galbraith, *The New Industrial State*, Houghton Mifflin Company, 1967, p. 173.
4. John Dewey, *op. cit.*, p. 117.
5. V. I. Lenin, *State and Revolution*, reprinted in *Communism, Fascism and Democracy*, edited by Carl Cohen, Random House, 1962, p. 186.
6. Karl Marx and Friedrich Engels, "The Communist Manifesto," reprinted in *Communism, Fascism and Democracy*, p. 108.
7. John K. Galbraith, *The New Industrial State*, Houghton Mifflin Company, 1967, p. 2.
8. Paul Ramsey, *The Just War*, Charles Scribner's Sons, 1968, p. 38.
9. Barbara Ward, *The Lopsided World*, W. W. Norton & Company, 1968, p. 92.
10. Fred J. Cook, *What So Proudly We Hailed*, Prentice-Hall, 1968, p. 251.
11. Richard Lowenthal, "The Logic of One-Party Rule," in *Russia Under Khrushchev*, 1962, p. 31.
12. Owen Harries, "Should the U.S. Withdraw from Asia," in *Foreign Affairs*, October 1968, Vol. 47, p. 23.
13. Paul Ramsey, *op. cit.*, p. 38.
14. See Herman Kahn, *Thinking About the Unthinkable*, Horizon Press, 1962, Chapter 8, and also Henry A. Kissinger, *Nuclear Weapons and Foreign Policy*, Harper, 1957, chapters 3 and 4.
15. Bertrand Russell, *Has Man a Future?*, Simon and Schuster, 1962, p. 73.
16. Mulford Sibley, "What About Unilateral Disarmament?," in *Seeds of Liberation*, edited by Paul Goodman, George Braziller, 1964, p. 88.
17. Carl Kaysen, "Keeping the Strategic Balance," in *Foreign Affairs*, July 1968, Vol. 46, p. 665.
18. Paul Ramsey, *op cit.*, p. 272.
19. Henry A. Kissinger, *op. cit.*, p. 135.
20. Paul Ramsey, *op. cit.*, p. 191.
21. *Ibid.*, p. 27.

148   CONTEMPORARY PROBLEMS OF DEMOCRACY

22. Henry A. Kissinger, *op. cit.*, p. 210.
23. Paul Ramsey, *op. Cit.*, pp. 427–428.
24. Herman Kahn, "If Negotiations Fail," in *Foreign Affairs*, July 1968, Vol. 46, p. 630.
25. Robert L. Heilbroner, "The Revolution of Rising Expectations: Rhetoric and Reality," in *Struggle Against History*, edited by Neal D. Houghton, Washington Square Press, 1968, pp. 118–119.
26. Robert L. Heilbroner, *op. cit.*, p. 121.
27. Charles W. Yost, "World Order and American Responsibility," in *Foreign Affairs*, October 1968, Vol. 47, p. 9.
28. Young Hum Kim, "Toward a Rational View of China: The Viet Nam War," in *Struggle Against History*, p. 215.

INDEX

149